THE
ADAPTABLE
HOUSE

THE ADAPTABLE HOUSE

Designing Homes for Change

AVI FRIEDMAN

McGraw-Hill

New York   Chicago   San Francisco
Lisbon   London   Madrid   Mexico City
Milan   New Delhi   San Juan   Seoul
Singapore   Sydney   Toronto

Cataloging-in-Publication Data is on file with the Library of Congress

McGraw-Hill

A Division of The McGraw·Hill Companies

1 2 3 4 5 6 7 8 9 0   DOC/DOC   0 9 8 7 6 5 4 3 2

ISBN 0-07-137746-8

The sponsoring editor for this book was Cary Sullivan, the editing liaison was Daina Penikas, and the production supervisor was Sherri Souffrance. It was set in Trade Gothic by North Market Street Graphics.

R. R. Donnelley & Sons Company was printer and binder.

McGraw-Hill books are available at special quantity discounts to use as premiums and sales promotions, or for use in corporate training programs. For more information, please write to the Director of Special Sales, McGraw-Hill, 2 Penn Plaza, New York, NY 10121-2298. Or contact your local bookstore.

 This book is printed on recycled, acid-free paper containing a minimum of 50% recycled, deinked fiber.

To Sorel, Paloma, and Ben

CONTENTS

A conflict exists between the dynamic nature of people's lives and the homes in which they choose to reside. As household members grow older, their habits, lifestyles, and use of space change. Yet residents often tend to regard the physical environment in which these changes occur—the home—as unchangeable. Altering a dwelling layout by demolishing partitions and building new ones, upgrading a home's heating system, and/or changing the location of the stairs in a building are seen as complicated and costly tasks to be avoided. People would rather change their own habits or move than undertake such work.

The argument that this book puts forward is that achieving a close fit between the evolving space needs of occupants and their homes ought to be simpler than it is at present. Residences can be designed and constructed to become life-cycle houses where changes are achievable and ongoing. More choices should be offered to buyers prior to moving in, as should the opportunities to adapt their homes with a minimum of difficulty during their subsequent residency.

Recent decades have provided ample reasons for considering a greater range of choices and adaptability in home design and construction. Demographic diversity and the rise in the number of nontraditional households that one currently finds among buyer groups is one such reason. Medical advances that have extended peoples' lives have created the need for designs that enable occupants to age comfortably at home. The emergence of new lifestyles and the rise of the work-at-home phenomenon have introduced uncommon design challenges. The continuing introduction of new domestic technologies, combined with excess consumption, have required residents to continuously upgrade dated systems. Environmental concerns and the need to design homes and communities that conserve valuable resources have made designers see another facet of adaptability: nature. An argument for long-term adaptability also has to do with increased mobility. During the life cycle of a typical North American wood-frame home, eight different households, each with its own unique characteristics, will reside in the dwelling. Designs should accommodate the needs of subsequent buyers as well as the original ones. These concerns necessitate a bold and fresh viewpoint of societal phenomena and practices as a basis for launching innovative design ideas. This book therefore provides a systematic guide to the conception and construction of adaptable homes.

Scholars and practitioners of architecture have investigated and designed both concepts and homes that provide their occupants with greater preoccupancy choice and the opportunity for later adaptability. The starting point for adaptable housing in modern architecture in Europe was Mies van der Rohe's steel-frame house built for the Stuttgart Exhibition in 1927, in which the inner walls could be located according to the preferences of the tenants. In both North America and Europe, the aftermath of the Second World War generated many concepts and techniques for such housing in low-rise, wood-frame, and medium-rise concrete structures. Unfortunately, when society entered a more prosperous era and buyers could afford larger homes, these ideas were largely abandoned. The accelerated ongoing changes previously noted make the need to revisit these ideas and designs relevant.

Innovation in building technology and products makes their reintroduction simpler. One of these innovations is the distinction between the structural envelope and the contents of the home. A reduction in the use of bearing partitions in the interior and an increase in the number of premanufactured components have provided the opportunity for greater choice and adaptability in design and construction. Home buyers can now assume a greater role in shaping their homes and can regard their contents, whether a room or a component, as items to select from in a catalogue. This book therefore sees knowledge about current practices in home design and construction, as well as available products, as an essential first step in introducing new ones. Descriptions and illustrations of designs and products have accordingly been woven into the text.

The introduction of designs and techniques that have expanded the realm of choice and adaptability in homes has to be accompanied by a parallel new perception on the part of builders and occupants alike. Seeing homes as places that permit constant intervention and modification requires a new vision as well. This book sketches such a vision and process. It suggests that new strategies need to be a combination of design approaches, an imaginative sequence of tasks, and innovative products. When these elements are combined, a coherent and systematic process, which in the past occurred at random, will take place.

The book is divided into three parts. The first part (Chapters 1 through 3) sets the stage for adaptability, the second (Chapters 4 and 5) outlines relevant principles, and the last (Chapter 6) shows their applications. Chapter 1 presents current motives for adaptability in housing. It also provides definitions and a framework within which the subject is discussed and explored. A look back to the roots and historical evolution of adaptability in North America and Europe, and in particular the post–World-War-II era follows in Chapter 2. Notable examples of low- and mid-rise buildings are discussed and illustrated. Present practices of a typical North American building firm are then introduced in Chapter 3. The author explains how innovative ideas and products are considered, adapted, or rejected by builders. The chapter also attempts to sketch a view of upcoming trends in home design and construction.

The second part is a systematic guide for designers and builders of adaptable residences. Chapter 4 deals with large-scale issues related to urban and building design. Selecting a suitable building typology, considering the home's dimensions, access and circulation, facade design, growth, as well as the building's structure and assembly are some of the issues explored. Chapter 5 invites the reader to step indoors. Aspects that touch on small-scale design issues are discussed. Functional zones, spatial configurations and strategies, as well as access and circulation between or within spaces are elaborated. The chapter moves on to deal with the function of rooms, growth and division of spaces, and the building's sub-components. The description ranges from access to utilities to surface finishes. Both chapters are graphically illustrated and show how adaptability can be better achieved in each of the subjects.

The third part (Chapter 6) applies the previously noted principles to practice. Several projects that have been designed and some constructed with choice and adaptability in mind are presented. Each project addresses different societal challenges. Responding to demographic and lifestyle diversity is dealt with in the first. Integrating new building technology and process and, in particular, prefabrication is the subject of the second project. Designing communities and homes that adapt to a site's natural conditions is discussed in the following project. Adapting to the needs of people with deteriorating health conditions as a result of disability and aging is dealt with in the fourth and last project.

A final guiding principle: although adaptability is referred to here as a building concept, it is first and foremost a state of mind. The need to see human habitations in a constant flux, along with changes in the lives of their inhabitants, is a primary notion in this book.

ACKNOWLEDGMENTS

Designing homes that enable occupants to adapt their interiors to varying needs has become a central theme of my architectural research and practice over the years. This book is the culmination of a process that was preceded by writing and building. Numerous colleagues and students have taken part in these endeavors and have inspired my thought processes. I would like to thank them all. Many also took part in the genesis and production of this book. Thanks to Nadia Meratla, Effie Bouras, and André Majaes, who helped with background research and data collection. To Michelle Kwok and Barbora Vokac for patiently producing the ink drawings. To Rem Garavito for creating the digital images. His dedication is much appreciated. To Jack Goldsmith for his help with photography, and in particular for recording the Next Home and St. Nicolas projects. To Masayoshi Noguchi for his assistance in translating from Japanese into English.

My thanks to the Next Home design team: Jasmin S. Fréchette, Doug Raphael, and Cyrus M. Bilimoria, who produced and photographed all the models shown here; Julia Bourke, who participated in the research and writing of the urban design and facade sections of the report, and to David Krawitz. David participated in and contributed to this book in many ways, including typing, editing, and scanning the graphic material and text. His help is much appreciated and admired.

Finally, my appreciation to my colleagues at the McGill School of Architecture and to the members of my family from near and far for their patience and understanding.

THE ADAPTABLE HOUSE

When the term *adaptability* in housing is mentioned, the tendency of both professionals and the public is to associate its application with technical advances. One design that comes to mind is that of a rotating home with openings that adjust toward the sun. Others might think about movable interior partitions that change position with the push of a button. Misconceptions about adaptability are the outcome of the term's many definitions and interpretations. *Providing occupants with forms and means that facilitate a fit between their space needs and the constraints of their homes either before or after occupancy* is one interpretation. The search for such a fit is the result of accelerated demographic, economic, lifestyle, and technological changes in society that have created a need for designers, builders, and buyers to inquire about adaptable housing forms.

KEEPING UP WITH CHANGES

In a society marked by constant change, it is difficult to make accurate predictions. Forecasting future demographic tendencies and national economic performance, identifying technologies that will revolutionize industry and business, or naming lifestyle trends that will predominate are challenging and sometimes nearly impossible tasks. Forecasting with any precision how homes will be designed and constructed in the future is no exception. However, we can anticipate that homes will continue to mirror the tastes, habits, and lifestyles of the people who inhabit them and that they will be influenced by new technologies yet to be introduced. And, as the pace of change in society inevitably accelerates and intensifies, so will the forces acting on how we occupy, utilize, and modify our dwellings.

The adaption of shelters by their residents to suit their varying needs has always been a part of human habitation. When societies were nomadic, the ability to adapt was relatively easy, since the dwelling carried by the dweller from site to site was light and simple. When more space was needed, it was easy to construct another tent or hut, then dismantle it and move on. When people settled, however, dwelling conditions naturally changed. Permanent walls now marked the boundaries of homes. Since interior and exterior walls could not easily be altered, adaptability took on a slower pace. In addition, extended families in both eastern and western societies commonly shared space. A single dwelling was commonly a residence for several households. Homes were inhabited and used by generations of the same family. They often doubled as living and work spaces either on one or two levels. Gradual modifications happened over a long period of time. When a member of the family died, his or her place in the home was taken by another. Physical changes such as the demolition of a partition wall or the addition of another level were limited to the constraints of the dwelling itself, the available space, and the skills of the builders.

The Industrial Revolution marked a turning point in many social structures, including habitat. People abandoned an agrarian way of life and left land that had been cultivated for generations to seek work in urban centers. The process also transformed the composition of the family unit, and along with it, the home. Homes ceased to be the domain of extended families. The concept of mobility also emerged. People moved to and settled where work was available.

Old towns and villages and the homes within them, like the city of Jerusalem, evolved by accretion over centuries.

Homes were no longer the residence of several generations, and they were purchased and sold when circumstances warranted. Adaptability took on a different meaning when homeowners could now find more fitting solutions for their space needs in another residence. Several aspects have influenced habitat: technology emerged as a driving force of building construction, and rapid urbanization drew even more people from the countryside to the city.

The end of the Second World War marked another turning point. Society began to undergo an accelerated pace of change. The proliferation of the automobile gave rise to the suburbs. The introduction of reliable forms of birth control affected the size of families, and the influential power of the media and consumerism affected home life. Some of these changes resulted in demographic transformations, accelerated technological evolution, and new lifestyle tendencies. In the twenty-first century, society, it seems, has become accustomed to the fact that constant changes are inevitable. These changes necessitate a new design paradigm in which future dwellings need to be more adaptable to the dynamic nature of societal trends and, as a result, their occupants' lives.

The conditions that have brought about a need for housing adaptability are, in fact, a result of a fundamental paradox. Homes are designed and built at a particular point in time, characterized by particular tendencies and technologies. As time progresses, the factors and decisions that shaped the original design become increasingly dated. A process of keeping up with change—either in the lives of the occupants or in the realm of technological innovation—inevitably begins upon occupancy. Some of the relevant conditions that have brought about the need for spatial change in homes are described in the text that follows.

Family Transformations

A good place to recall changes and their effect on the domestic environment is society itself. The transformation of the traditional family which formerly con-

In the post–World War II period, builders catered to the needs of traditional families, who constituted the majority of home buyers.

stituted the bulk of North America's home buyers is one of the key factors that drives the need for adaptable housing. Immediately after the Second World War, builders had little difficulty identifying the demographic makeup of their clients. Breadwinner dad, stay-at-home mom, and their children resided in a limited number of housing prototypes. Bungalow, rancher, or two-story styles were common forms of housing for everybody. Home builders offered designs that fitted a preconceived notion of how families used space.

Other family compositions began to emerge in the later decades of the twentieth century. With changes in moral values and the acceptance of nonfamily unions and same-sex marriages, the definition of *family* was expanded. They were all potential home buyers, and designers and builders had to respond to

Presence						
Morning	Noon	Afternoon	Early Evening	Late Evening	Night

(Table: "Typical use – examples" — pictographic diagrams illustrating family activities across the times of day.)

A currently outdated version of the interaction between family members and their activities was portrayed in *The Dwelling* by Deilmann, Kirschenmann, and Pfeiffer in 1973. The table shows the mother spending the day at home attending to the children's needs. The father returns in the evening to complete the predictable daily cycle of nuclear family activities.

their unique lifestyles and living habits. Furthermore, the same dwelling unit will now have to accommodate a wide range of households over its life span. For example, childless couples who work at home need separate offices in addition to common sleeping quarters. Young couples who purchase a home may need one bedroom at first, but later, as their families expand, will need additional space. Two unrelated people who wish to share the cost of buying and maintaining a home may buy a unit and will look for a two-suite arrangement in a single house, each suite with its own bedroom and bathroom.

The institution of marriage was also eroded in the twentieth century. The incidence of divorce increased significantly, as have the number of single-parent households. The most dynamic of all family arrangements is the progressive transition between different forms of family status. Marrying, having children, getting divorced, and then remarrying require spatial arrangements that permit the move from one status to another if the household wishes to remain in the same residence.

The process is further complicated by the transformation of children from toddlers to young adults. Each step in a growing process requires physical adjust-

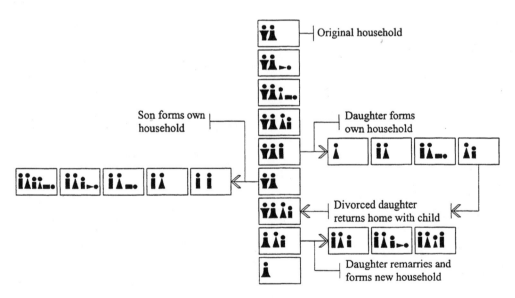

Adaptable homes need to be able to respond to a situation commonly occurring nowadays where a child grows up and leaves the original household to form his or her own household, but then, after divorce, may return later to the original household, only to remarry and leave again.

ment. The space arrangements in homes with a small child are different from those in homes with teenagers who seek a greater degree of privacy. Their in-house mobility may take them from a space within or adjacent to their parents' bedroom to a room in the attic or basement. With the expansion of communication technologies and the availability of information appliances with targeted content for each family member, the levels of interaction and intimacy within the household have declined. Adaptability to ongoing space needs that result from growing up in this age requires a new conceptual model for housing.

Preparing for Old Age

A notable sign of scientific and societal progress is the advancement in the field of medicine. Men and women now live longer. A lot longer, in fact. It is projected that on the average, men and women will live well into their eighties. By the year 2030, those 65 years and older will constitute 20 percent of the entire population (Riche 1986). Governments, it seems, will not likely be able to provide institutional care for many. Obtaining appropriate housing, therefore, is anticipated to become one of the most important issues to occupy the elderly.

Several housing solutions are available to seniors. Some might decide to continue to live in their houses after the kids have left to form their own households. Last-time buyers might move into smaller units and others into retirement communities where they are cared for socially and medically. Regardless of what the choice is, surveys consistently show that the elderly prefer to age at home independently rather than end their lives in an institution. Their residences, therefore, have to be adapted to the aging process.

It is a slow process. If retirement begins at 55 for some, and they are expected to live into their eighties, they will need to occupy themselves for 25 to 30 years. Experts see several aging stages within this period. Seniors will move from being young-old (55 to 60 years) to old-old (85 to 90 years) (Carstens 1992). During that time, the mental skills of many seniors will deteriorate. There will be a parallel decline of motor abilities. Adapting homes has to reconcile both aspects.

Big and small changes in homes are commonly taking place. Guest rooms with an adjacent bathroom are built to host visiting offspring and their families. Young retirees who embark on a sign-off career convert empty rooms into offices with much electronic equipment. Sunrooms with skylights are built to help perk up low feelings and loneliness. In some homes, bathrooms assume a therapeutic role, with multijet shower stalls with adjustable seats and whirlpool baths to help with aching bones. Bathtubs with grab bars and side doors to prevent slipping are also becoming common. Some bedrooms have a medical station installed. New technologies now permit those in need of constant medical supervision to have their vital signs checked with a special kit and sent electronically to a clinic, and then carry on a conversation with a nurse through a computer. Exercise rooms with advanced brands of machines help the elderly to stay fit and to keep their muscles stretched.

The aging process is often accommodated by the installation of a range of building products. Easy-grip door handles provide convenience for arthritis sufferers, and nonslip flooring increases safety in homes with frail occupants. Designing homes to accommodate the needs of an aging population requires the adoption of a design strategy and construction practices that let occupants modify and fit their homes when needed.

Adaptability of a dwelling for the aged can involve large-scale changes, or small ones, such as the installation of grab bars, or a bathtub equipped with a door.

Avoiding Unnecessary Mobility

In comparison with the populations of most other continents, North Americans have a high rate of mobility. A household moves every 10 years on average. If one considers the useful life of a home to be 100 years, it is likely that each house will accommodate 10 different households over the course of its life cycle. Changing residential location can be the result of getting a new job, social upgrading, or a desire to live closer to other family members. Sometimes, however, the home itself can be the cause of moving. Such reasons could include lack of space for a growing family, a change in family status, or the desire to have a new interior arrangement. Often the tendency is to relocate rather than to adapt.

Relocation results in significant transaction costs. These include legal fees, additional resources spent on selling the old home and purchasing the new one, expenditures on moving companies, and the cost of fitting the new home. Adaptation and expansion of the original dwelling may vastly outweigh relocation costs as a solution to the multitude of changing needs within the household. Adaptability as a part of the housing process can therefore be viewed as a viable alternative to the complexities and expense of relocation. Built-in design principles or technologies permit the occupants to undertake ongoing changes to the layout of the home and the components within it.

The amount of required space fluctuates according to life-cycle stage. A young couple without children, for example, will need less space than a household with two teenagers. When the children leave to form their own households, unoccupied rooms are left in the empty nest. At the time of retirement, there is also frequently a decline in income. Homes can therefore be designed so that a portion of their space can be segmented to become an independent dwelling unit for rental and supplemental income purposes.

Fitting New Technologies

When homes are designed and built, their architects and builders incorporate into them the technology of their time of building. In the ensuing years, new advances are introduced and old technologies become obsolete. Unlike systems and utilities in office buildings that are designed to be upgraded and adapted to the needs of the original and subsequent tenants, residential construction

The evolution of plumbing systems provides an argument for the need to design homes that can keep up with changes in technology. At the turn of the twentieth century, nickel-plated, enameled iron pipes were installed outside the wall. A tin-lined pipe that combined the durability of lead with the purity of tin was used to prevent poisoning. The use of galvanized steel pipe was subsequently introduced and later abandoned, as it was found to be subject to rust. Rigid copper pipes that were introduced at the same time were also expensive and hard to handle. New trends and practices led to the installation of plumbing in the walls themselves. The 1950s saw a proliferation of soft copper pipes for water supply and cast iron for drainage. Lightweight PVC pipe was introduced in the 1960s. This was ideal for drain and vent pipes, relatively inexpensive, and much easier to install and connect. Flexible pipes were introduced and became common in the 1990s. They were made possible by the invention of a unique, durable plastic called cross-linked polyethylene, formulated specifically to withstand high temperature and pressure (Ou 1999).

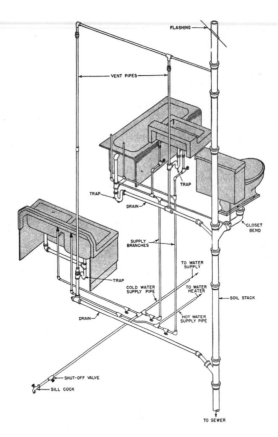

House plumbing system at the beginning of the twentieth century.

rarely permits such intervention. Increasing acoustic insulation levels, installing new wiring, or replacing a plumbing or heating system demands major intervention on the part of the renovator, resulting in large expenses and inconvenience for the occupants. Designing homes that permit and simplify constant renovation and upgrading can extend the home's useful life.

New technologies were the catalysts for the introduction of new uses in homes. The reorganization of the North American job market and advances in the field of communications were behind the emergence of the home office for full- or part-time work. The development of the fax machine and electronic mail has expanded the reach of homes. A portion of the space that had earlier been used for domestic purposes has been converted to business activities. It is ironic that new technology has reintroduced the work/live environment that was part of the human habitat centuries ago. Nowadays many new homes are fitted at the time of construction with computer cables and jacks in most rooms. It is more costly, however, and a much greater technical challenge to install new wiring in existing structures.

It is hard to predict what will be the ultimate effect of information appliances on homes, now that all members of the household already have their own systems. New uses already point in far-reaching directions. Communication between homes and health-care centers, distant education, and entertainment à la carte are growing uses for homes. With new technologies anticipated, residents will most likely require constant adaptability of both functions and utilities.

Affording in Stages

Affording a home is a challenge for families with fewer means, and in particular for first-time home buyers. Reductions of subsidies and public housing starts by governments in many cities have encouraged the intervention and exploration of cost-reduction strategies by private-sector builders who wish to take advantage of the demand for affordable housing. One of these strategies is progressive occupancy. Purchasing a home where part of the space will remain unbuilt or unfinished in return for a lower cost is common in many parts of the world. The process can be planned in advance, allowing work to occur without an interruption in family life. Decisions as to how, when, and what the functions of the spaces might be can remain flexible, for the homeowner to determine.

The unfinished space could be in a basement level, any of the floors, or in the attic. Space can be also be added on to the original structure, whereby a small unit can be built initially, to be expanded later on. Designing for adaptability as a result of future expansion will facilitate the "growing process," whether it is inward or outward.

PROCESSES OF ADAPTABILITY

A basic interpretation of housing adaptability is the *refitting of a physical environment as the result of a new circumstance.* This process can be brought about by conditions that are internal or external to the dwelling, some of which have already been described. The fitting of a home can occur prior to occupancy, as a choice offered to buyers, or after the first or subsequent occupants have moved in. Researchers distinguished between several stages in which adaptability can take place in the life cycle of a building (Oxman 1977). The first stage is *initial design,* where the designer employs strategies and components during the conception phase to facilitate pre- or postoccupancy adaptability. The second stage is *construction,* where the builder exercises the option of deciding on the project's main characteristics—for example, the number, types, and sizes of units—as well as a range of choices to be offered to buyers. The third stage is *use,* where, during occupancy, the homeowners exercise the previously conceived and constructed options for adaptability in the unit.

Design

Design for adaptability begins with a systematic evaluation of aspects related to the home's interior and the relation between a single dwelling unit and groups of homes. The process of including adaptability during the design phase is different in a custom-design process, where the occupant's identity is known, than that followed in a tract-housing development. When the custom design of a home begins, architects acquaint themselves with the client's specific requirements while preparing the program. In conversation with the future occupants, the designer collects information on the number and sizes of rooms needed, desired layout arrangement, style, the preferred quality of finishes, and budget.

At the end of the process, the design reflects the expressed needs of the client whose wishes will be accommodated *prior to moving in.*

Adapting the design to clients' needs prior to occupancy is harder in tract housing since the identity of the occupants is unknown. The architect designs for a developer who provides a sketchy profile of a potential buyer, as well as a budgetary target. The number of rooms, layout, and type of finishing preferred by this unknown occupant are all assumed. It is a process that requires foresight and forecasting. Providing clients of custom-designed or tract homes with choices and adapting the unit to their needs or budgets prior to moving in is referred to here as *design for preoccupancy adaptability.*

The search for a methodological approach to preoccupancy adaptability in modern architecture began as a result of the need to accommodate the requirements of the occupants in housing despite the fact that their specific characteristics were unknown. These beginnings can be traced to Europe in the period following the Second World War when homogeneity in mid-rise, mass-produced housing dominated the urban scene (Rabeneck et al. 1973). The proposed methods and building systems attempted to allow occupants to personalize both the exterior and the interior of the dwellings and will be outlined in the discussion that follows.

Another aspect of the custom-design process of homes by architects is an attempt to anticipate the future needs of occupants and to design for them. The clients often indicate some of their future plans: a young couple's desire to expand their family, for example, and as a result, to turn a study into a child's room, or to finish the attic that will be left bare at first. It is a process of predicting and forecasting events in the life of a household and responding to them by creating potential scenarios that relate to particular solutions. The architect then proposes a design that responds to the need for postoccupancy adaptability, allowing the occupants to fit their homes to their evolving needs.

Allowing for postoccupancy adaptability in the production of mass housing is naturally a tougher undertaking. The architect must assume not only the profile of the occupants but their evolving needs. The chosen design strategy, for example, might be to provide open spaces or to install building components that simplify the process of modification when it happens. Incorporating strategies and building systems into homes to permit occupants to adapt them to their evolving space needs or budgets is referred to as *design for postoccupancy adaptability.*

The traditional residential design and construction process often tends to ignore the occupants' evolving needs. When designers draw up plans, the rooms have clear and defined functions. The uses are marked on the drawings themselves: *master bedroom, bedroom,* or *kitchen.* To further clarify these notations, architects also draw furniture to provide a sense of scale for the space.

Several characteristics that restrict easy adaptability and functional change in homes are spaces that are generally designed for only one function and are difficult to use for any other purpose. Room proportions that are in keeping with a single intended room function will also be difficult to adapt to other uses. Rooms that are provided with function-related fixtures and fittings (such as closets in bedrooms) will limit adaptability, as well as lighting and socket outlets that are located according to the planned function of the room, for example, lighting related to bed position. When windows are designed to reflect the function of each room—such as small windows in bedrooms—they will also hamper adaptability. Other restricting elements are access to rooms other than

A single window in a bedroom will restrict the division of the room into two spaces

the living room by way of a narrow, minimal hall which cannot be used for any purpose other than circulation; single-door access to all rooms; outdoor space accessible from the living room only; and relationships between rooms that are generally based on the shortest distance between associated functions, such as the kitchen next to the dining room, and the bathroom next to the master bedroom (Rabeneck 1974a).

Construction

Adaptability during construction refers to the employment of strategies or building components that enable the builder or the occupant to make changes to the design as the project's building progresses. In tract developments, it allows the builders to offer choices to buyers. They can select between alternative layouts for the same dwelling size or fixtures that they wish to include with their chosen design.

Changes during construction are common. As market conditions change, and the builder realizes that clients other than those anticipated are expressing interest in the project, new designs can be offered or the layouts of existing units can be changed. In a custom-design project, clients might change their minds about a space or a choice previously made, once the construction is in progress.

Use

Once the occupants move into their new home, a life-cycle process that generates ongoing needs for adaptability begins. It might take on simple forms such as painting, expanding the kitchen, or demolishing a wall separating two rooms. The process could be more elaborate, involving the joining of two levels or building an addition. The need for adaptability might be driven by *functional* reasons, such as the desire to have the home function in accordance with space needs triggered by change in the family life cycle. A bedroom, for example, could be converted to a hobby room following the departure of a grown-up son or daughter. Adapting homes can also be the result of moving to an existing dwelling as a subsequent occupant. The need to modify will result in reshaping a place that was designed and fitted over the years to the needs of another household. Adapting a dwelling need not be restricted to the interior of a unit.

Over time, change can be made to the building envelope. The change may depend on modifications to the interior. A sunroom, for example, can be constructed while changes are made to the kitchen, or be independent of it, like building a deck.

FORMS OF ADAPTABILITY

Strategies for the adaptability of homes can be integrated into the design *before* construction begins. They can take several forms, each with its own unique characteristics, opportunities, and constraints. Forms of adaptability depend on many factors, among them the type of home, the method of construction, and the procedure used to make the changes. Achieving adaptability could be the result of changing the character of an entire building or simply a component of it. Four main areas of intervention have been identified as critical to achieving adaptability in a dwelling:

1. *Manipulation of volumes,* which refers to the considerations that a designer, builder, or occupant will give to the use of the entire volume, such as all the floors of a multistory building.
2. *Spatial arrangement,* which considers the way in which the spaces themselves within the volume are dealt with and used. A space can be an entire floor or a single room on that floor.
3. *Growth and division,* which refers to design strategies or means that permit the expansion or reduction of volumes or space either during design and construction or later throughout the occupancy.
4. *Manipulation of subcomponents,* which are the elements employed in the construction and use of a building, which can be as large as structural components or as small as a water pipe.

Manipulation of Volumes

Manipulating volumes is a manifestation of dwelling adaptability, which could be combining several floors to make a larger unit, then dividing it at a later stage. A single-family dwelling on several levels, for example, can become homes for several households, each on a single level or part of one. In order for such a process to occur, the designer must consider elements that limit the conversion, such as the location of circulation areas and utilities. Changes to volumes could also require alteration of the building envelope which, as a result, could change its appearance.

Spatial Arrangement

A range of design strategies can allow adaptability of space within a home's volume prior to or following occupancy. One of these strategies, for example, is to propose a room that can accommodate multiple uses, such as a living room, an office, or a bedroom. Another manifestation of adaptability would be the need to accommodate an elderly person who may be confined to a wheelchair and require special interior arrangements. The entire layout, for example, could be modified to create a suite within the home for an around-the-clock personal nurse, or adjusting the dining part of the kitchen.

Adapting spaces can also be achieved by using furnishings. The initial design could anticipate such a process by creating appropriate dimensions for storage spaces. A hide-a-bed, for example, can turn a living room into a bedroom. A set of bookshelves can serve as the divider between the living and dining spaces in one large room.

Growth and Division

Design that considers expansion beyond the dwelling (add-on) or growth into a space within the perimeter of the original volume (add-in) is another form of adaptability. The process could also be reversed and a large home could be divided to form two dwelling units. On a smaller scale, expansion could take place within the space itself. Taking advantage of unused area under a staircase or enclosing an alcove and turning it into a room is also a form of expansion. The added space needs to be designed to function along with the existing one. In the event of a division, the new spaces need to be designed to function independently. The designer must pay attention to issues such as natural light and to circulation between the old area and the addition, among other considerations.

Manipulation of Subcomponents

Subcomponents are the elements that are fitted into the house once the structure has been erected and prior to the closing of the horizontal and vertical surfaces. Recent advances in information technology, for example, have introduced additional and different kinds of subcomponents into homes. They can be electrical or computer wiring, heating and ventilation ducts, kitchen and bathroom fixtures, and prefabricated facade elements. The useful life of many such components is often shorter than the life of the house's structure, which requires replacement when the part is obsolete. Designing for adaptability would permit easy access and replacement when the subcomponents need repair or upgrading.

Design for adaptability and for the evolving needs of occupants in dwellings has been attempted before. The return of millions of veterans in North America and the ensuing baby boom of the 1940s and 1950s, coupled with the stagnant state of the housing industry as an aftereffect of the Depression years, created a housing crisis of great magnitude. This crisis stimulated research into innovative design and building technology and resulted in the development of strategies appropriate to small, affordable, and adaptable homes.

In Europe, the devastation inflicted by the Second World War prompted the need to house a large portion of the population efficiently and cost-effectively. Conventional mass housing strategies were challenged by theorists who proposed to transcend the notion that homeowners were simply consumers, and, instead, respond to the diverse needs of the individual. The monotony and uniformity of mass housing induced architects to restructure these systems by providing inhabitants with the opportunity to influence the design according to their particular personal requirements and play an active role in the housing process. Furthermore, not only was the diversity of needs acknowledged, but subsequently the recognition of evolving needs was also built into these strategies.

Prosperity in North America enabled buyers to afford larger homes, and the lack of a continuing pursuit of new technologies and forward-looking design ideas led to the abandonment of flexible building strategies. In Europe, minimal government financial support brought an end to many competitions and building initiatives that advocated adaptability and user participation. Examining and reflecting upon various initiatives, ideas, and projects developed in North America and Europe are valuable toward integrating adaptability as a pertinent element in the future.

POST–WORLD WAR II NORTH AMERICA

With the return of Second World War veterans, households that had placed their aspirations on hold during wartime frugality began to search for housing with revitalized optimism and purpose. Homes, however, were in dire circumstances as demand vastly outweighed supply. The magnitude of this crucial lack in availability was further exacerbated by the 1946-to-1960 postwar baby boom, which played a key role in dictating the market housing type. There was also a severe shortage of supplies and materials for construction, initially brought about by the economic stagnation of the Depression and further aggravated by wartime shortages of skilled labor. A second factor was the predicament of excessive overcrowding and the enforced communal living of family and non-family groups. By 1945, many homes situated in large cities were deemed severely substandard and in critical need of exterior and interior repair. Basic amenities such as communal flush toilets and bathing facilities were significantly deficient.

In that same year, numerous associations were established in North America as vehicles to alleviate this housing shortage. Radical transformations of the housing industry were undertaken as various levels of government launched economic proposals to expedite the pace of development. Not only did these organizations help finance new developments, they also established limits on the price and size of subsidized homes. Furthermore, rigid control was mandated on style and form, resulting in the promotion of conformity to a conservative prototype. Implicit in these confining restrictions were significant ramifications with respect to the effect they had on design strategies. Such constraints compelled architects and builders to experiment and investigate innovative cost-reduction strategies as well as to attempt to respond to the needs of the occupants with maximum efficiency while building to lower size standards. Essentially, stringent government regulations provided a foundation of affordability that established adaptability as a criterion in the diligent and efficient planning of these homes.

During the postwar euphoria, both consumer demand and expectations were substantial, born of rejuvenated optimistic convictions. The public consensus placed high hopes on incorporating the latest in technology, planning, building, and labor-saving devices as critical elements of the design program. Consequently, the postwar housing industry dealt with two underlying realities. Primarily, traditional design and construction methods were no longer feasible practicalities in affordability considerations. Second, significant savings and efficiency in small-house construction were accrued not from major items but from meticulous attention to innumerable details and alternatives. As a direct result of both the price and design restrictions, architects were obliged to reorient their practices away from the traditional, ornate, and stylish dream houses that had preceded the disruption inflicted by the Second World War on North American society, and to satisfy the high demand and flagrant optimism of a new order. This impact was translated into functional, practical, economical, and adaptable solutions appropriate to the dynamic needs of a family home.

The form and style of postwar housing was dictated in part by the economic conditions of the time and resulted in a redefined notion of the home. Though labor and materials were costly, land was cheap, and this led to distinct prototype developments. Government-sponsored homeownership initiatives argued for the continued preference for the single-family house, while the pervasiveness of the automobile, the proliferation of new highways, improved standards of living, and the ready availability of inexpensive land spurred the exodus to the suburbs. The increasing numbers of young families with several children fueled this suburban development; these families wanted low-density, family-oriented housing that could easily be adapted to their changing needs, equipped with backyards and open spaces (Friedman 1995).

MASS PRODUCING WITH CHOICE

In their quest for cost reduction, architects readily welcomed the idea of mass-producing housing and actively sought to implement a variety of cost-reduction design strategies. The war had already introduced industrialists to the concept of full-scale mass production, and many war factories were converted into producing innovative materials that were less costly yet extremely efficient for a growing construction market. The average house had doubled in price by the 1940s and therefore the fundamental need to maintain low construction costs directly stimulated the development of new building materials and products: prefabricated window units, weather-resistant exterior plywood, latex glues and caulking, composition-board products, and improved drywall construction merchandise. The astounding demand for housing placed tremendous pressure on builders to improve their speed and efficiency, leading to valuable technological breakthroughs and the implementation of adaptability as a means to satisfy the requirements of a population that was expanding dramatically; one example of such a breakthrough was the notion of prefabricating units as whole products. Despite the valid potential demonstrated by the prefabricated unit in meeting high demands efficiently, the production of the unit in substantial quantities proved to be too cumbersome and costly. Instead, prefabricated housing components such as wood studs or kitchen cabinets were deemed more economical, and *Architectural Forum* (1951b) reported that by 1951 one-fifth of an average house was made of prefabricated components. Windows, doors, and wall panels

---

William and Alfred Levitt developed a comprehensive and very successful approach to mass-produced housing by introducing the assembly-line production system into the housing industry. The institution of power tools and labor specialization at the construction site is attributed to the Levitts. Self-described as the General Motors of the housing industry, the Levitts divided housing construction into 26 steps, with extensive use of prefabricated components. The resulting implications of this carefully controlled production methodology was that an 800-square-foot (80-square-meter) house was completed every 15 minutes. The Levitts produced their own nails and concrete blocks; they owned lumber mills and distributing firms for electrical appliances. They strove to maximize the efficiency of the house construction process, and also capitalized on the economies of scale available to a developer capable of building. The Long Island development where people stood in line to buy houses was dubbed "Levittown" and was indeed a homogenous mass of mass-produced housing, preplanned and standardized. The majority of these components were prefabricated en masse and assembled by carpenters on site who specialized in a particular installation. However, adapting production methods was evident in the option available to buyers to select from several facades for the same layout which manifested some choice and alternatives to suit buyer preferences. The design was sold as a complete package with all the modern conveniences. The Levitts were able to purchase materials and appliances at a discount, and the houses came equipped with such items as built-in televisions, washing machines, kitchen appliances, and sliding aluminum windows. These homes were designed with features intended to make a small home prestigious. Such features included a carport with outdoor storage space, additional storage space in the unfinished attic, tiled bathroom walls, flush doors, sandstone-colored bathroom fixtures (as opposed to the standard white), and bookcases built into the brick fireplace wall (*Architectural Forum* 1950a).

were also standardized and produced in large quantities to efficiently reduce costs. Breaking down the process of house construction into subcomponents meant an increase of choice and greater potential for adaptability as a design strategy. In some projects, buyers were allowed to participate in various degrees in selecting the finishes to their homes.

Multipurpose Rooms

Another important strategy that maximized the efficient use of space and kept housing prices low was the use of a square or rectangular floor plan with as few interior subdivisions as possible. Economy was achieved through the square

In the Levitt House (1950 model), four different facade options were offered to buyers of an 800-square-foot (80-square-meter) home. Mass production of a limited number of models was the reason behind this offer of choice.

floor plan, since it minimized the amount of materials required for foundation walls and insulation. It was also substantially cheaper to service, due to lower heating costs resulting from more efficient surface area exposure. Other cost-saving techniques used by builders were the introduction of multipurpose rooms, the elimination of the basement to reduce excavation costs for the foundation, back-to-back location of kitchens and bathrooms to minimize work for plumbing, centralized heating to reduce ductwork, and various built-ins to save space. In the elimination of many extraneous traditional rooms, adaptability was used as a design strategy to incorporate multiple activities within a limited amount of space.

Open Spaces

The improved living environment was essentially a reevaluation of the conventional housing form restrained by the demands of affordability. Modifications implemented in this reevaluation resulted in the elimination of the traditional second story, staircase, dining room, extra bathroom, cellar, attic, stylistic trimmings, millwork, and decorative shutters. Several strategies were employed to provide functional houses without compromising livability. These strategies called for a reorganization of traditional house planning and embodied adaptability as a means to accommodate the present and future demands of the inhabitants. The living room was expanded to increase its flexibility as an all-purpose space. While maintaining traditional functions, the living room acquired the diverse functions of the study, dining room, parlor, and playroom. The kitchen was no longer relegated to the rear of the house but was integrated into this multifunctional living area. In form, it was transformed into a pragmatic U-shaped work space equipped with practical appliances and gadgets. A low counter was the only division between the kitchen and living area, transforming the kitchen from its traditional service purpose into a practical, adaptable, and efficient utility space that not only accommodated culinary services but enabled clear supervision of children playing and facilitated the serving of meals by being adjacent to the dining area.

The scarcity of interior space and the dynamic needs of the family resulted in the reduction of such fixed features as walls that would instill rigidity in the plan and counteract the notion of adaptability these homes embodied. The objective of maximizing the potential range of uses within

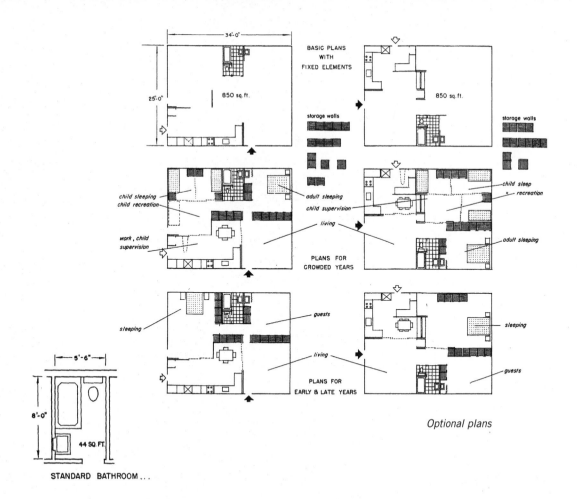

BASIC PLANS
WITH
FIXED ELEMENTS

34'-0"

25'-0"

850 sq.ft.

850 sq.ft.

storage walls

storage walls

child sleeping
child recreation

adult sleeping

child supervision

child sleep
" recreation

work, child
supervision

living

adult sleeping

PLANS FOR
CROWDED YEARS

sleeping

guests

sleeping

living

PLANS FOR
EARLY & LATE YEARS

guests

Optional plans

5'-6"

8'-0"

44 SQ. FT.

STANDARD BATHROOM...

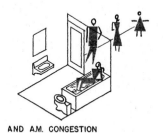

AND A.M. CONGESTION

In 1950, the architect Haydn Philips interviewed residents of Levittown to determine the interior space needs of the postwar nuclear family, and designed a flexible plan intended to adapt to changing needs over time. Instead of fixed partitions, modular closets and folding partition walls are provided which can be arranged according to the particular needs of the users.

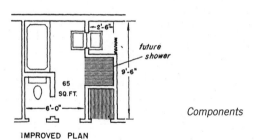

2'-6"

future
shower

9'-6"

65
SQ.FT.

6'-0"

Components

IMPROVED PLAN

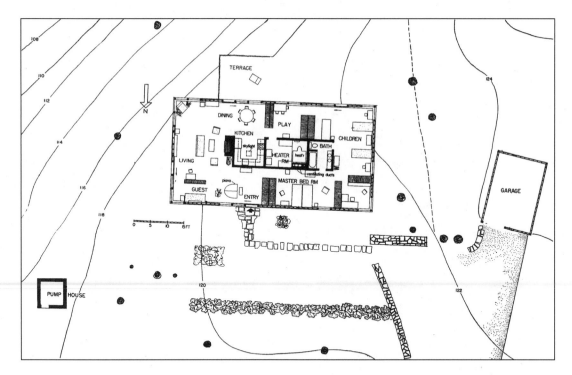

In 1951 Vincent Scully Jr. designed a 1891-square-foot (189-square-meter) one-room house in New Haven, Connecticut. The open-space design strategy was meant to create a simple and functional space for a family of five without being "overfinished in meaningless ways and overgadgeted."

restricted interior space was accomplished by presenting an open floor plan that allowed the occupants to define the space according to their specific requirements, as opposed to the designer dictating the definition of the space. Rooms could be easily transformed as required with the implementation of innovative features such as sliding walls and movable partitions that allowed privacy levels to be modified and rooms to be created or merged at the discretion of the residents.

Space-Making Devices

The prime challenge in incorporating diverse functions into a small area was to design with a conscious effort to maintain an ambience of spaciousness and detract from the impression of a small house. An emphasis on relating the

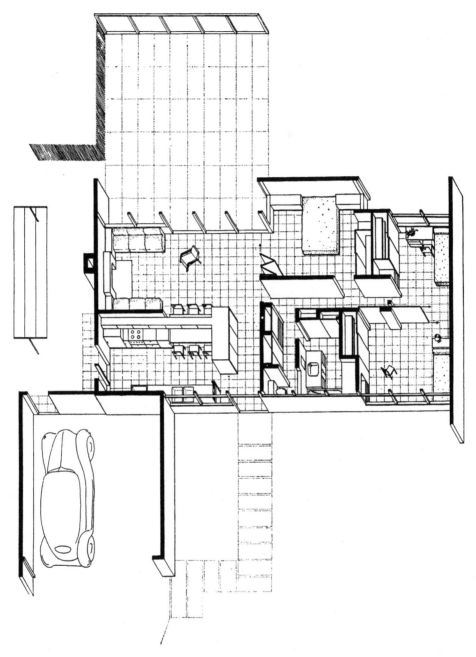

In this 1949 convertible plan, accordion and rotating partitions were used by Gregory Ain in Los Angeles to provide flexibility in the bedroom areas. The partition systems are fixed but allows for a combination of uses. The medium-sized bedroom can serve as an addition to the multipurpose room, while the two small bedrooms can serve as single large one.

house to its immediate surroundings was one such strategy commonly employed to instill the illusion of greater living expanses. Large plate-glass windows and patio doors dissolved the confining impression of conventional walls and instead extended the perceived limits of the internal rooms into the exterior. Another strategy involved using drapery, accordion walls, or ceiling-high movable storage shelves as partitions. Consequently, the finite limits of the rooms were blurred, which cultivated an enhanced milieu of larger internal rooms. However, the development of outdoor living at this time was also the result of the quest for efficiency. The use of well-designed outdoor rooms not only expanded the dimensions of the home, but they were also not subject to the constraints of government size regulations.

Adapting through Expansion

It is evident that size reduction was not compatible with the postwar living environment. Living space was systematically and intensely subjected to a reevaluation process in order to identify the essential spatial requirements of a small unit and maximize its adaptability. Despite the spatial limits, the majority of occupants ventured to have more than the essential living room, kitchen and two bedrooms. Therefore, designers were presented with the added challenge of overcoming the limits of the home's envelope and integrating the prospect of expansion to accommodate the flux of needs surrounding a maturing family. For many homeowners, a small home represented a short-term housing solution but in no way did it adequately satisfy any permanent objectives. In order to avoid the high cost of relocating, many families began to examine lower-cost alternatives. In the interest of responding to these requirements, designers developed strategies both to allow for expansion within the original house and to facilitate easy additions. Design for adaptability and expansion represented a considerable departure from the preconceived floor plans of traditional design and emerged as an innovative strategy to increase the suitability of a small home to the dynamic of the family by explicitly recognizing the potential for individuals to design and alter the living environment to cater to their evolving needs.

Two types of homes were built across North America during the period: wartime houses and small-lot housing. The wartime house was built during a

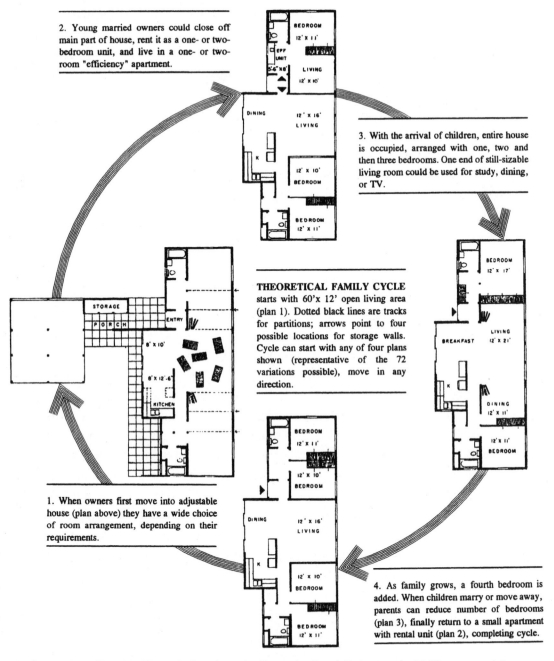

2. Young married owners could close off main part of house, rent it as a one- or two-bedroom unit, and live in a one- or two-room "efficiency" apartment.

3. With the arrival of children, entire house is occupied, arranged with one, two and then three bedrooms. One end of still-sizable living room could be used for study, dining, or TV.

THEORETICAL FAMILY CYCLE starts with 60'x 12' open living area (plan 1). Dotted black lines are tracks for partitions; arrows point to four possible locations for storage walls. Cycle can start with any of four plans shown (representative of the 72 variations possible), move in any direction.

1. When owners first move into adjustable house (plan above) they have a wide choice of room arrangement, depending on their requirements.

4. As family grows, a fourth bedroom is added. When children marry or move away, parents can reduce number of bedrooms (plan 3), finally return to a small apartment with rental unit (plan 2), completing cycle.

The focus of the Flexabilt Home in San Antonio, Texas, by Frank Robertson in 1952 was on adding or subtracting rooms within the fixed perimeter of the original house. The single-family house allowed 72 variations on one floor plan, using movable closets and retractable walls which ran from floor to ceiling and which could be arranged by residents without carpentry.

period when land was cheap and plentiful, and therefore each unit was granted ample outdoor living space. Owners could add extra rooms in the rear of the dwelling without compromising their private outdoor space. Small-lot housing did not share this same adaptability of horizontal expansion; apart from vertical growth, there were very few options in expanding these homes. Furthermore, the square plan of the wartime home provided far more adaptability in the incorporation of additional rooms.

Most wartime homes were adjusted over the years to meet the needs of each household. In making adaptations, the owners either had to have some building skills of their own or they had to contract professional renovators. Without such a commitment and investment, these homes, particularly the bungalow, could not adequately meet the changing needs of the households. The interior layout of the wartime house was modified primarily to accommodate the need for more storage. The kitchen was the area where most renovations were made or desired, followed by the children's bedrooms. The coal shed in the rear was one of the most versatile areas in the wartime house in meeting the changing spatial needs of the household; it was generally adapted for use as additional living space. Storage problems were resolved by employing unused spaces in the home such as the hollow area beneath a staircase.

As North America moved away from the immediate postwar era into the prosperous 1950s and 1960s, the need for adaptable and expandable housing strategies subsided. Buyers had the means to afford larger homes and builders were eager to build them. Gradually, the expansion of lot sizes and housing standards eliminated the need to efficiently utilize small spaces. The building industry fell into a traditional conservative pattern where an acceptable limited number of house types was the norm and innovative ideas such as adaptability were regarded as unnecessary frills.

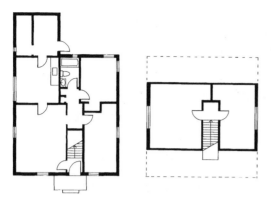

Original plan: ground floor (left), upper (right)

Original plan

Modified plan A: ground floor (left), upper (right)

Modified plan A

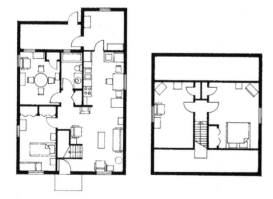

Modified plan B: ground floor (left), upper (right)

Modified plan B

Changes made by occupants to wartime homes in Montreal, Canada: two-story (left) and one-story (right).

DESIGN FOR CHOICE AND ADAPTABILITY IN EUROPE

After the devastation of the Second World War and the ensuing population expansion, housing activity in Europe was dominated by a high rate of production. In contrast to the North American dilemma, the European housing crisis had the added dimension of densely populated areas with a strong urban tradition of mid-rise, multiunit housing. The greater the number of people who had to share a given amount of space, the more complex the problem became. In the postwar European scenario, the individual dwelling unit was clustered, resulting in a significant need for a more intricate interweaving of spaces and functions. European urban developments were typically mid-rise, high-density, concrete structures, which was a direct contrast to the low-rise, low-density, wood-frame suburban projects of North America. One strategy commonly employed by Europeans to arrive at a solution was the mass-housing development which actively eliminated the identity of both the dwelling and the occupant.

For most people living in Europe's metropolitan areas, single-family houses were luxuries and multifamily complexes were affordable. Subsequently, the highly-centralized housing industry, brought about by government subsidies and standards, provided the foundation for the requisite mass production of housing and imperative industrialization. In order to radically increase the housing stock to fight the severe shortage, governments encouraged the development of building systems as part of a general policy. This highly centralized and controlled effort resulted in the production of large urban areas of monotonous and uniform buildings which erased any trace of individuality or character from the urban environment and alienated the occupants who inhabited such repetitious and depressing structures. Architects became increasingly alarmed by the results of the government initiatives, yet continued to be swayed by the affordability of more industrialized systems. Bound by government regulations and building systems, architects saw an ever-widening gap between their expectations and the actual results. Consequently, decisive initiatives were instigated to respond to the needs of the public and to humanize housing developments within the framework established by the government.

In an effort to alleviate the monotony both for the individual occupants and for the benefit of the urban fabric, architects began to elicit alternative measures to mass housing, but were nonetheless bound by government regulations. It was assumed that the alienated element in large-scale production was the individual dweller who had not been considered as an active participant in the housing process. Since it was not possible to think in terms of separate lots and individual houses in an urban, high-density environment and to attain affordability, multifamily developments, whether low-rise or high-rise, had to contain numerous dwelling units. In this type of urban predicament, architects proposed redirecting the housing effort toward the large-scale building of generalized infrastructures, sensitized to the urban context, and the industrialized production of an infill system to acknowledge and accommodate the diverse needs of the occupants, and add the critical degree of adaptability long-removed from mass housing (Habraken 1972).

The design strategy of mass housing was conventionally based on the floor plan or unit plan which was simply repeated throughout the building. In a situation in which costs had to be minimized and government standards and codes followed, the basic floor plan was usually a compromise, the result of complex negotiations between architect, client, builder, structural engineer, and an array of other professionals. However, architects began to design the individual units as repetitive elements with the added capacity for adaptation and the ability to comply with the particular needs of the occupants. In an attempt to humanize the social housing built, two concepts of adaptability evolved. The initial concept concerned *preoccupancy adaptability* in which developed units were adjusted to the occupants' lifestyles prior to their arrival. This was soon followed by *postoccupancy adaptability,* which enabled the occupants to modify the units upon moving in.

Providing pre- and post-occupancy adaptability was a result of the principle of hierarchy. It was a key idea in contemporary housing design in which a relationship was established between the physical supporting structure of columns or bearing walls and internal subsystems within dwellings. The separation of housing into two complementary sets of hierarchically organized subsystems, each of which is physically independent, has been a contributing factor in the development of adaptable housing systems which provide a variety of housing designs, adaptability to change, and occupant participation in the design process (Oxman et al. 1984).

An analysis of completed projects demonstrates the extent to which adaptability was used in the development of mass housing. Together these

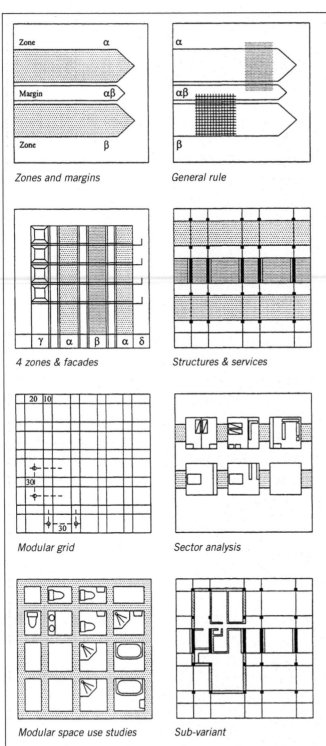

Zones and margins

General rule

4 zones & facades

Structures & services

Modular grid

Sector analysis

Modular space use studies

Sub-variant

In 1965 a Dutch architect named John Habraken introduced a design methodology to enhance occupant choice and adaptability. This methodology was characterized by nonstructural "Infill" assembled by the occupant in "Zones and Margins" within a general "Support" structure. The facades similarly varied according to internal design and broke the monotony of traditional mass housing production. Support, in its simplest form, included the structural skeleton of the dwellings whereas infill contained any combination of partition, drain, waste, ventilation, water supply, heating, electrical, data and communication networks, equipment, fixtures, wall, floor, cabinet, and ceiling systems. The method systematically divided the Support into spaces designated as Zones, Margins, and Sectors, that are a precise means of delineating territory of similar location and dimension in the Infill. Each zone was specifically commissioned for diverse uses in relation to their functional and locational suitability. The margins—smaller-dimensioned spaces interposing two adjacent zones—were utilized to augment the possibility of greater depth requirements provided it had not previously been assigned a prior use. A sector, on the other hand, is an area appointed to incorporate one or more zones and margins which could prospectively be planned and evaluated. Together, these classified systems combine to create various permutations of unit configurations recognizing the individuality of the occupant's needs (Dluhosch 1974).

Schematic principles of Habraken's support and infill methodology.

projects exemplify the impact of innovation on the reduction of monotony in conventional European mass housing and the restoration of individuality in design.

Adaptability in Mid- and High-Rise Buildings

Unité d'habitation in Marseille, France, was a prototypical design that acknowledged the diversity of needs inherent in each occupant. Built in 1946, Le Corbusier's 18-story design was based on four basic spatial modules which were varied up to three levels and three parallel units to permit a variety of apartment sizes and layouts. Except for one-room apartments, all units were maisonettes, with adaptable open plans and terraces to maximize the spatial qualities of a small unit. The apartments followed a consistent zoning relation between light penetration and the depth of the room. Living rooms were always two stories high, opening toward the outside. The bathrooms and kitchen were oriented toward the central corridor. Built-in movable partitions permitted the division of a children's bedroom into two distinct spaces.

In Sweden, adaptable housing has been promoted by the National Association of Tenants Savings and Building Societies. Typical of these developments were the apartments at Uppsala, built in 1964. This project, by architect Axel Grape, contained 16 apartments of three different sizes on four floors serviced by two staircases and elevators. The building used a system of large-panel concrete construction, with load-bearing external walls and crosswalls with an intermediate row of columns giving a relatively unobstructed floor area to each unit. In many of the configurations developed, the columns served as space-defining elements, acting as anchors for movable cupboards and casework. In all units, services such as ventilation, water supply, and drainage were assembled along the wall backing the stairwell.

In the two years following completion, 12 of the occupants had modified their partition layouts (4 prior to occupancy), and 3 had changed their configuration more than once. Direct feedback from the occupants suggested the main advantages to be variation of number, size, shape, and position of rooms, and also the connection and demarcation between rooms. Modifications indicated a tendency toward more open planning, resulting in only bedrooms remaining fully enclosed.

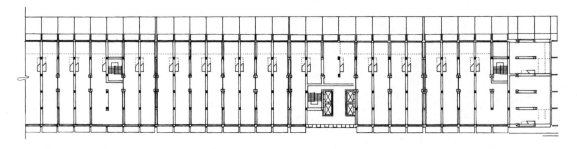

Plan

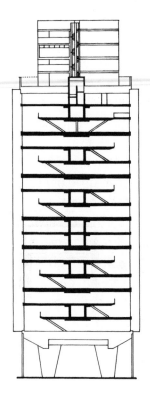

Section

Le Corbusier's Unité d'habitation offered different unit sizes to accommodate a range of households in the preoccupancy stage. Allowances were made for unit adaptability after moving in.

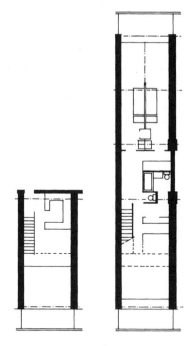

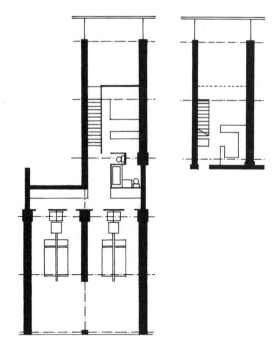

A 980 sq. ft. (98 m²) maisonette for a family with 2 to 4 children

A 1,370 sq. ft. (137 m²) maisonette for a family with 4 to 8 children

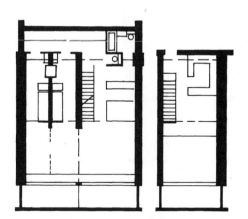

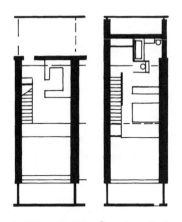

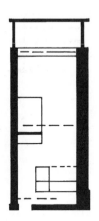

A 980 sq. ft. (98 m²) maisonette for a family with 2 to 4 children.

A 590 sq. ft. (59 m²) maisonette for 2 people

A 325 sq. ft. (32.5 m²) flat for a single person

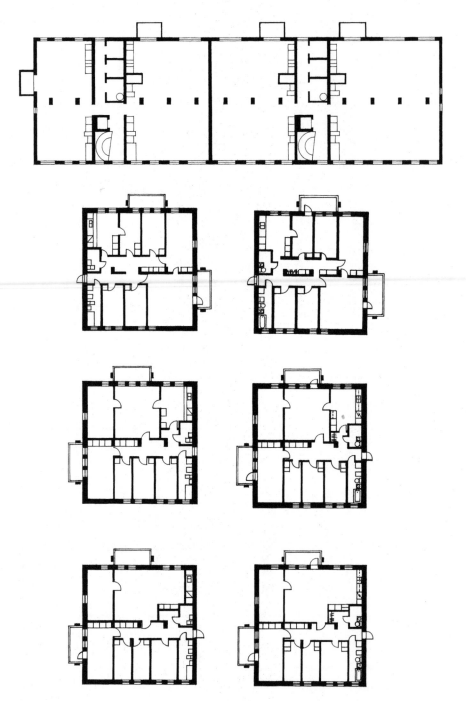

The 1964 Diset project in Uppsala, Sweden, featured 16 apartments of 3 different sizes (top).
The load-bearing external wall permitted occupant choice prior to moving in, as well as adaptability at the postoccupancy stage (bottom).

Preoccupancy Choices

The Hollabrunn project in Austria, which won a competition in 1971, applied Habraken's methodology to offer maximum choice and scope for participation by the occupants while respecting cost limits and conventional technology. The problem stated by the competition, which was entitled "Design Without Information," called for more efficient design for future clients whose exact needs were unknown. This led to a general planning strategy for the design of a project characterized by open zones within a general support structure to accommodate occupant-chosen layouts of various types, sizes, and materials, including variable facade treatment (Dirisamer et al. 1976).

The beginning of the actual construction phase coincided with regular meetings attended by occupants, architects, and representatives of the housing cooperative, in which detailed information was distributed to all participants. This information pertained to dwelling size and type, possible configurations, costs, construction schedules, and "blank" tartan-grid floor plans with only the structure and location of vertical service elements shown. When requested, samples of floor plans were available to assist occupants in the development of an individual layout. Additionally, a scale model of the project was displayed and progressively developed in order to illustrate construction progress three-dimensionally. This allowed the participants to better visualize their own decisions and be part of the entire development process.

Adaptability in Low-Rise Units

A system of zones and margins, also based on Habraken's methodology, was implemented in the government-sponsored Primary Support Structure and Housing Assembly Kit (PSSHAK) project in England. The structural system employed in the project was based on a 12-inch (30-cm) module between walls and a thickness of 12 inches (30 cm) for structural concrete walls. A variety of products and manufacturing companies were involved in this hierarchically organized project, with the internal component kits manufactured in Holland and installed by British contractors. The range of design variations chosen by the occupants reflected the needs of a cross section of the population more faithfully than any attempt by traditional mass housing. Out of a total of 45

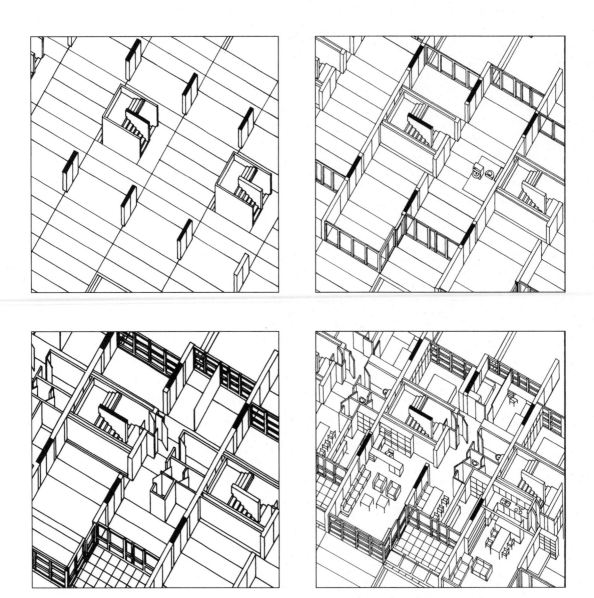

Support structure in Hollabrunn, Austria. Concrete structures of slabs and columns were systematically aligned to a module of feet (510/960 cm), and the tartan grid of ⅜ inches (10/20 cm) was applied to the interior arrangement of material and spaces.

Key

LR	Living room
BR	Bedroom
K	Kitchen
WC	Toilet
B	Bathroom
S	Storage
Bal	Balcony

Examples of floor plans designed by the occupants for the same envelope in Hollabrunn, Austria. The openness of the support structure was utilized effectively, enabling individual configurations.

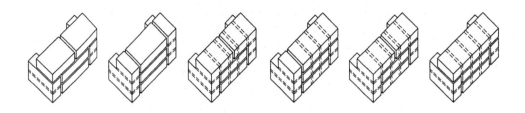

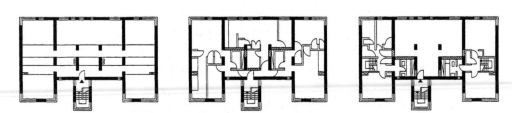

In the Primary Support Structure and Housing Assembly Kit (PSSHAK) project in England, the structure was designed to be divided according to the space needs of the occupants (top). They were also given an opportunity to design their own interiors (bottom).

dwelling units, only 2 or 3 were identical. The system also had the potential of redesigning dwellings to suit a household's changing needs, but this was subject to technical limitations and political and economic constraints relating to government housing policy. In spite of its relatively small size (45 units), the project demonstrated an economic and architectural realization of the occupants' continuous intervention with the home in initial and progressive stages of development. Preoccupancy participation in PSSHAK showed that it was possible to discuss the needs and expectations of future occupants with the architects during the design stages of a scheme (Ravetz 1980).

Interior and Exterior Variations

The Montereau project in France in 1971 was an attempt to incorporate adaptability in a mid-rise apartment building containing 36 units, the plans and elevations of which could be selected by the occupants. The objective of this experiment was a postoccupancy observation of how the families utilized the

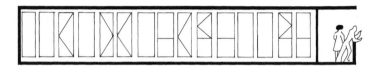

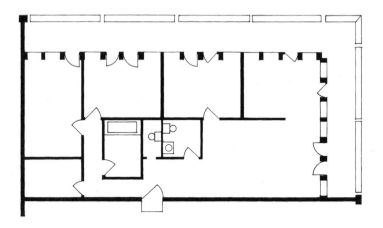

Unit and facade A

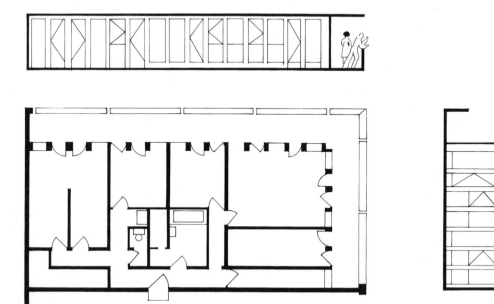

Unit and facade B

Two plans and facades of units designed by the occupants of the Montereau Project in France. The occupants developed plans that were not only fitted to their initial requirements but also allowed evolution of the unit according to the family's evolving space needs.

space that had been arranged individually according to their specifications. The structure was designed with minimum internal supports on a 36-inch (90-cm) grid in order to maximize adaptability. The architects, Arsène-Henri Frères, attempted to provide the occupants with the satisfaction of living in a personalized home that further recognized their evolving needs.

To allow optimal freedom in the arrangement of internal partitions, the floor slabs were built with a minimum number of supports: the central core, the party walls between the apartments, the technical ducts in each unit, and on the perimeter by concrete posts at 36-inch (90-cm) centers. Only the entrance door and the technical duct of each apartment were specifically designated by the architect. Service rooms, such as the bathroom and kitchen, were connected to three faces of the central technical duct; the fourth face was reserved for a linen-drying closet automatically ventilated through a central system. Central heating was adopted using small convection radiators located between the perimeter posts. These heating elements could be individually controlled to allow the apartments to be heated efficiently without inhibiting the planning freedom. Movable partitions could, in theory, be positioned at any grid point in the module with ample provision of electrical outlet sockets at the 36-inch (90-cm) intervals. The overall open area of each apartment was 893 square feet (89 square meters) and this surface was increased to 1235 square feet (123 square meters) if the balcony that runs the full length of the apartment face was included. The facades were designed to correlate with the plan and tastes of the occupant, using five types of components which were fixed between the structural columns. These included solid fixed panels, glazed fixed panels, French doors, or a choice of fixed and opening windows (Martel and Ignazi 1974).

Movable Partitions

In Carasso, Switzerland, architect Luigi Snozzi installed high-quality movable partitions, originally designed for office buildings, into a residential context to provide a greater degree of adaptability in the 1973 project Casa Patriziale di Carasso Ti. The idea of installing commercial steel partitions was an inventive transfer of a sophisticated product from one market to another. Considerable attention was also paid to the location of service cores within the 12-apartment complex. The apartments were standardized for 4-½ and 6-½ room units and

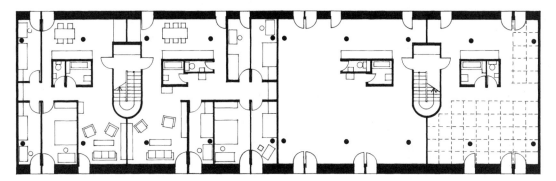

In the Casa Patriziale di Carasso Ti project in Switzerland, adaptability was facilitated by installing movable partitions. The floor plan shows an empty shell (right) and the interior arrangements of two units (left).

were freely grouped around this service core. The implementation of commercial steel partitions was well received, and a postoccupancy study reflected no attempt by occupants to apply wallpaper or paint over the baked-on matte acrylic finish, indicating the apparent acceptance and success of such adaptation (Rabeneck et al. 1973).

Adaptability through Floor Systems

Another application related to the Support and Infill design method was made by John Habraken through the Matura Infill System. This system is made of a prefabricated package of off-the-shelf subsystems and parts that are integrated into two elements: the Matrix Tile and the Baseboard Profile. These components provide adaptability in design, fast on-site installation, and future changeability in concrete building. The Matrix Tile is basically a modular floor panel that has grooves in it to provide room for distribution of primary building services such as drains, water, heating, electricity, and all kinds of pipes and wiring. The Baseboard is the secondary distribution system that runs wires for appliances. The Matura system allowed for quick installation and a wider choice of floor plans (Kendall 1996).

Design for adaptability experienced relative success in the European housing market as a result of several advantages, including comprehensive political

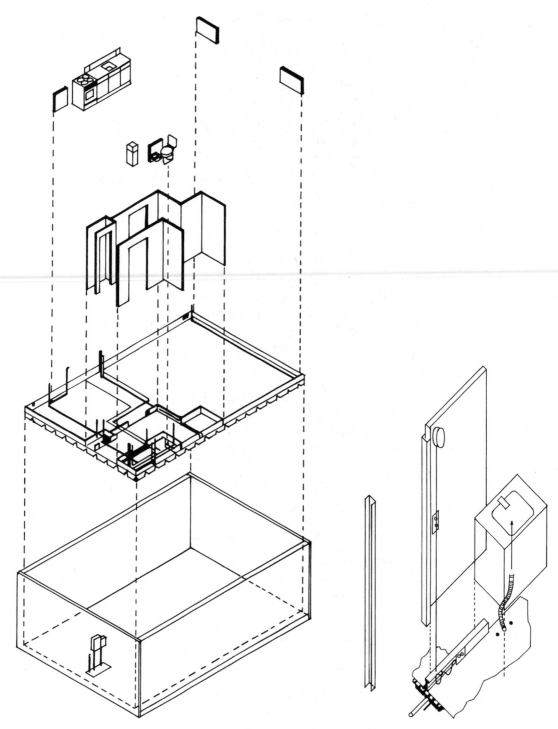

By using a Matrix Tile (left) and a Baseboard Profile (right), the Matura Infill System permits adaptability to occupants' needs in the pre- and postoccupancy stages.

motivation, active government intervention through the initiation of national competitions, and subsidy of housing projects. Furthermore, lower rates of residential mobility encouraged continuous intervention of householders in their dwellings. Modular coordination was another pertinent variable characteristic of adaptable developments. In order to efficiently accommodate future occupants, anonymous in the conceptualization phase, this systematic approach simplifies the extent of the internal configurations and ensures compatibility with the structure. In many instances, however, technical complexity deterred occupants from maximizing the full potential of such components.

Fragmented in structure and vulnerable to negative economic trends, the North American home-building industry has persistently cultivated a self-defense mechanism that has impeded its departure from traditional conventions. Conservative by nature, builders have exercised great caution when assessing new techniques or products that may be created in response to contemporary demographic and economic factors as prime influences of design. A certain degree of choice and adaptability is nonetheless offered by merchant builders to enhance the marketability of their homes. And several indicators suggest that societal trends will finally lead to significant changes in residential design and construction practices in the years to come.

THE HOME-BUILDING FIRM

The home-building industry is pivotal to the vitality of the North American economy. More than a million housing units are built annually, and in a good year this number can exceed two million units. The amount spent on single-family house construction accounts for 30 percent of the money spent each year on all building construction activities. The industry also accounts for the creation of a large number of annual and permanent jobs. It is estimated that in addition to contributing indirectly to local economic prosperity, the construction of each house generates two annual direct jobs.

When compared with other industries of the same magnitude, it seems that the home-building industry is slow to adopt innovations. Whereas the computer, biomedical, or auto manufacturing industries, for example, overhaul production methods or introduce new products frequently, the home-building industry somehow lags behind. This stands in marked contrast to characteristics that were prevalent during the 1940s and 1950s and that led to the development of numerous housing concepts and to the emergence of an efficient organizational structure that remains intact today.

Offering choice to new-home buyers prior to moving in and designing for occupants' adaptability at the postoccupancy stage largely depend on private-sector builders. It is therefore important that the organizational patterns of the industry that led to a unique decision making process by its leaders be understood before attempting to introduce new design concepts or products.

Caution needs to be exercised when attempting to describe the home-building industry. It cannot be viewed as a homogeneous group. There are many small builders who each construct fewer than 10 units a year, and there are also several large firms that build more than 10,000 homes annually. There are custom-design builders who build exclusively to the specifications of clients and their architects, and there are tract builders who design and build developments whose future occupants and their tastes are unknown at the time of design. There are innovative builders who welcome new technologies, and there are conservative ones who avoid change. Yet several general characteristics govern them all.

North American development has been influenced by the continent's "frontier mentality." Fueled by population growth and economic expansion, North

Americans have persistently pushed back the frontier and replaced it with urban development. Ostensibly, mistakes had marginal consequences since the supply of virgin land seemed to be inexhaustible. Towns and cities emerged where the untouched hinterland once stood and streams were redirected to service developing rural and urban communities. Charged with the spirit of the time, engineers succeeded in linking the Pacific to the Atlantic with the steel technology of the railroad. Most important, the continent was irreversibly opened for mass immigration and urban development.

Prior to the Second World War, North American home-building firms consisted primarily of small teams of skilled carpenters who would build one house at a time for individual families, or on speculation, where the house would be completed before being sold. A comparatively lengthy construction period resulted from the fact that all housing components were manufactured on-site. When a home was custom-built, the builders respected the wishes of the client. Home design followed the style of the time, and adaptability was largely a result of having multipurpose spaces.

However, in their response to the housing shortage following the Second World War, home-building firms demonstrated that the sudden and overwhelming demand for housing could be efficiently supplied. Success was facilitated by the builders' access to large land tracts which allowed for economies of scale, publicly financed services, and the availability of low-cost mortgages to the average citizen. Clearly, homebuilding firms responded to this shortage of housing by organizing into systematic and efficient manufacturing teams. Home-building operations examined traditional homebuilding techniques and acknowledged the disorder, hours and days of downtime, and the imprecise nature of time allocation as to who was doing what and when. To merchant builders, the natural response to the housing shortage was a model comparable to a production line manufacturing automobiles—a highly mechanized production process where the product was stationary and the labor moved from home to home (Eichler 1982). Any new idea, method, or product that stood in the way of this efficient process was viewed with disfavor. Client choice, when offered, was often minimized to a limited number of models or finishing items.

The home construction process has emerged as an extremely fragmented mechanism, forming a pyramid in which multiple subtrades perform crucial tasks orchestrated by the builder. This enables merchant builders to obtain competitive prices for services from subtrades when required, while not having to

Tract housing development sites were organized to be highly efficient. The introduction of many prefabricated building components increased this efficiency as well as the adaptability of the units constructed.

keep them on permanent staff. The industry is particularly vulnerable to slow winter months in the Northeast and to economic recessions that force merchant builders to adjust the number of staff members they employ to balance with demand. For any given project, different subcontractors are used for electrical, plumbing, painting, carpentry, roofing, and foundation, to name a few. Several subtrades are further separated into more specialized divisions. For example, subcontractors specializing in carpentry work can be divided into those working at formwork, framing, flooring, or cabinets. The resulting implications of this specialization is that each subtrade operates as a team with different goals. Communication lines run from the builder to each subcontractor but not between the various subcontractors themselves. This process has turned the construction site into an assembly line, making it a streamlined and extremely efficient operation.

The introduction of a technique or process that slows down this efficient operation or disrupts a channel of communication between a builder and a subcontractor is likely to be rejected. Also, design that includes products that require the involvement of additional subtrades would not be welcomed.

Economic constraints imposed upon the home-building industry offer a better explanation for its lack of constant evolution and provision of adaptable solutions to homeowners. No other industry relies so heavily on the ready availability of credit, and this is clearly exemplified in the dramatic reduction in housing starts during conditions of financial constraint. Parallel to the economic limitations placed on the industry, home buyers face similar obstacles. The difficulty of obtaining a loan and high interest rates are two such factors which in the past have led to an inability on the part of home buyers to translate their needs for a home into a realized purchase. The resulting implications of this situation are that home builders often scale down production starts when economic restraints are anticipated. Lending institutions are also reluctant to finance projects that may appear too risky. A development in which a previously untried design concept or technique is offered will be carefully scrutinized by a banker.

Due to the economic environment in which home-building firms operate, and with the exception of a few very large companies, many firms are relatively small and often family controlled. Few managerial employees are engaged, as the majority of these positions are incorporated into the builder's own duties. These tasks pertain to responsibilities such as arranging financing, advertisements,

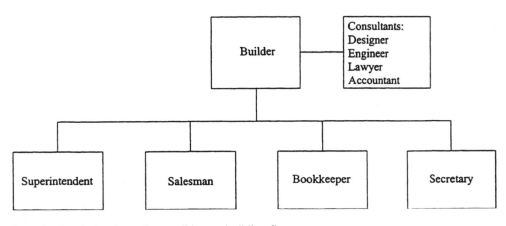

Organizational structure of a small home-building firm.

project management, and office tasks. Employees working for home-building firms are remarkably versatile, capable of performing more than one task efficiently. During times of economic slowdown, the firms operate with as few employees as one bookkeeper. This ability to operate with a low overhead cost is a remarkable aspect of homebuilding firms, and one that has ensured their survival. Yet some of these very characteristics have made firms reluctant to be open and accept innovative ideas that radically alter the way homes are built.

Despite behavioral characteristics that have hampered the home-building industry's ability to offer a wide array of choices at the preoccupancy stage, and strategies, techniques, and products that enhance adaptability throughout the residency, some degree of participation is permitted. Present practices are outlined on the pages that follow.

CURRENT CHOICES

A vital part of the builder's home delivery process is the ability to ensure a quick sale and proceed on to the next project. Attending to a client's request is a relatively simple matter in custom-built homes. The builder follows the architect's drawings. When the design calls for the incorporation of a design or technique that promotes adaptability, the builder naturally charges for expenses associated with materials and labor.

In tract housing, on the other hand, when the client's identity and preferences are unknown at the time of design, the model home holds a great deal of importance as a marketing device. It is the merchant builder's "store" that is visited by many potential clients. Merchant builders spend on average about four percent of the sale price for selling, model home presentation, and advertising (Eichler 1982). Taken to the highest level, efforts invested in model home presentation become very expensive. The building cost is financed by a construction loan, but there is no easy way to borrow money for landscaping, furnishings or displays. With minimal variation in the plans produced and few options available to cater to user needs, the model home is designed to entice potential buyers and provide them with an image of what their home may resemble.

When a tract housing project is initiated, several options are inherent in the marketing strategies of a home which offer a degree of choice and adaptability to

The model home is commonly furnished to make the interior attractive to an assumed average buyer.

the buyer. The model unit is displayed and promoted to potential inhabitants by a salesperson. Conventionally, model homes involve a precisely calculated manipulation of lighting effects, dramatic attention-grabbing appliances and furniture, and structured circulation through the sales office where glossy promotional material is exhibited to further lure clients. After visiting the model unit, clients may wish to purchase the home in its standard format—or propose modifications to the interior layout or exterior appearance. The scope and the range of choices offered to buyers depends on the degree to which the builder wishes to allow choice and adaptability. However, it is to the builder's advantage to limit choices and build identical and repetitive units in order to simplify the process of design and construction and therefore benefit from economies of scale.

As part of the routine purchasing process, the client is offered an array of interior finishings to choose from. Among these options are wall color, types of floor coverings, kitchen cabinet styles, light fixtures, and accessories through-

A typical new housing development displays a limited number of models and interior arrangements for buyers to choose from.

out the home. On a larger scale, in some projects buyers are allowed to change the interior layout, combine spaces, and add features (for example, add a powder room) according to their needs and budgets. In other projects, buyers are given the option of selecting from among limited variations of the same design or from different models. The available choice enables buyers to influence the unit's layout and appearance in the preoccupancy phase to a certain degree. Rarely, however, are building components or strategies offered to buyers to enable progressive modifications of homes according to the dynamic nature of diverse households. The sales representative attempts to satisfy the needs of the buyers at the time of purchase only.

The unique organizational structure and patterns of performance of a home-building firm need to be taken into consideration when innovative approaches or techniques are proposed. What one needs to bear in mind when "thinking outside the box" will be outlined in the next section.

A room in the sales office contains samples of finishes for choice by buyers.

INNOVATION IN HOME-BUILDING

A home builder who was once asked if he was interested in an idea that would reduce construction time, answered that he would be ready to implement any new idea with 20 years of practical experience. In fact, some suggest that it takes between 3 years ("overnight") to 15 years ("a mean time period") from the time a technique or product is introduced until it gains widespread acceptance (Sichelman 1987). The resistance to innovation—which refers to the introduction of new construction methods, building systems, and products that are not commonly used—impedes the ability of the industry to respond to buyers' changing needs. Prior to a review of innovative strategies and means for adaptability, one needs to examine the process of introducing new ideas, concepts, and techniques.

The person within the home-building firm who will most likely decide whether to use or to reject a new product or method will be the builder, that is, if one assumes that the technical information is reviewed carefully and time is actually invested in a discussion with the manufacturer's sales representative. The builder will then reflect on the impact that the invention will have on the delivery of his project. An innovator has therefore to consider the number and type of organizations that will proceed with implementing the product or method. Implementation that will require collaboration among several subcontractors, for example, will have less chance of being accepted due to the builder's prerogative to reduce coordination time. In addition, there are no contractual agreements between the subcontractors, as all feedback is directed straight to the builder (Roberts 1970).

The builder's objectives deserve analysis based on fundamental economic concerns. Builders' interests are to reduce construction and overhead costs and devote minimal means to post-sales maintenance (which is a weak point of the home-building industry). If these critical objectives are satisfied, and the innovation contributes to the building process, the builder will support the innovation. Another strategy that appeals to builders is the ability of the innovative product to act as a marketing device, to increase sales through the promotion of their firms as more advanced than the competition. The diffusion mechanism of innovation results from a process of technology

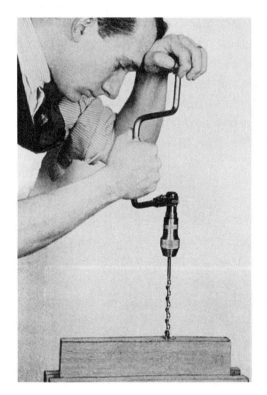

Over recent decades, numerous innovative tools and products have been introduced that simplify what were formerly labor-intensive tasks.

push and market pull. In order for an innovation to be diffused, there must be a demand for it.

Builders will consider implementing systems that promote adaptability in housing projects based upon the system's contribution to their objectives. One such advantage includes the ability to adapt the internal layout to cater to individuals without significantly increasing the cost of labor, time, and material in unsold units after project completion. Adaptability would also gain approval if it correlated with the adjustment or replacement of failed parts throughout the obligatory guarantee period or if the units sold faster by using adaptability as a marketing device.

It can generally be noted that the further the innovation moves from an established practice, the greater is the potential of the innovation to be rejected. Consequently, the introduction of innovation should not break down existing communication between parties nor suggest new contractual forms; it may, however, modify some conventions. An established and long-working relationship is evident between builders and highly specialized trades. For instance, builders will not press their carpenters to adopt new framing techniques for fear of losing them and sacrificing competent workers at the expense of speculative new ventures. However, if the carpenter's work can be replaced by another trade which markets a new framing idea in a complete supply and installation package, builders may assume the risk involved, particularly if they are confident that the "new" trade's work can be well-integrated into the overall process and coordinated with other trades.

The contribution of the invention to the objectives of the party who either needs to accept it or promote it is another attribute that an inventor has to consider. Support for a new material or method will be given only when it promotes the interests of the party that finances it. Thus, inventors should know in advance the precise objectives of the party to whom they offer the product. The specific objective of the products manufacturer, for example, is to increase sales. This is the only organization in the home-building industry that has sizeable investments and overheads in the form of production equipment, facilities, and promotion. Consequently, manufacturers' organizations are larger and their operations are more permanent than the builder. The home-building market is only one market for those manufacturers, in addition to the commercial building industry, and in most cases, pressure for technological innovation comes from this domain as well. Also, they have the means and the infrastructure to approach the homeowners themselves through regular marketing channels such as retail outlets or the media. It is therefore assumed that manufacturers in general will welcome an approach that opens the market for new products that have the potential of being purchased by users not only during construction but throughout the life of the building. Additionally, it seems that adaptability in North America can benefit from the well-established marketing research and sales which in the past successfully introduced a variety of innovative products into the homebuilding industry (Friedman 1989).

The successful introduction of concepts and systems that provide occupants with greater choice and adaptability throughout their residency will depend on demand by the home buyers themselves. They will also depend on the ability of the home-building industry to innovate and offer new ideas. It is

The nature of successful innovation in the home-building industry is easily recognized in the adoption of prefabricated roof trusses. Prior to their introduction, home builders used a joist and rafter system to support the roof. A series of joists were laid horizontally and nailed together, resting on the exterior load-bearing walls. Rafters were then nailed to the joists, which prevented the rafters from spreading. Roof construction was an extremely complicated and time-consuming procedure requiring skilled carpenters. Spurred by the postwar shortages of both materials and labor, home builders were forced to meet these challenges by becoming more efficient. Responding to these conditions, the necessary "pull" for innovation existed and resulted in the creation of the prefabricated roof truss. The introduction of this product was initially hampered by government safety concerns and building code legislation. However, in a 10-year period, the necessary tests to confirm the standards administered to the truss eventually gave rise to a higher-quality product and gained immense credibility with government sponsorship and certification. As a result of this innovation, the need for specialized roof carpenters was eliminated by the use of framing carpenters who were given directions from truss manufacturers for their installation. Also, roof trusses have eliminated the need to construct bearing walls for roof support and have provided a greater degree of interior flexibility. With the creation of a new manufacturing industry, the truss accommodated the operations of the home-building industry and relieved the amount of responsibility on the part of the builder (Sternthal 1993).

Prefabricated roof trusses.

generally noted that builders and subcontractors have a conservative approach toward innovation. However, once a particular product has been proven successful and is accepted, this conservative nature serves to ensure a long period of existence for the new product and thereby justify the effort invested in promotion.

HOME BUILDING IN CHANGING TIMES

Given the characteristics of a home-building firm, one might ask whether, how, and what forms of adaptability will be introduced in future homes. Several emerging factors attest to the fact that builders are responding to the need to change traditional customs and routines and to introduce a greater degree of innovation. Driven by societal trends and technological advances, one can expect considerable differences in the design and construction of future homes.

A key word to characterize transformations in the housing market is *diversity*: diversity of buyer groups, employment opportunities, lifestyles, and housing choices. Diversity influences the range of buyers searching for a home that best suits their household composition and means. Designs offered by architects and builders to married couples with children have to be different from those proposed to single-parent families with grown-up children. Demographic diversity requires attention to more than offering choice of wall color and floor covering during the selling of a home. Constructing a shell and assisting the occupants to participate in the design of their own interior arrangements might be one strategy to accommodate diverse buyers in the same project.

Several technological advances unrelated to home building have contributed to the need to update construction methods. Most of them are in the realm of communication technology. The proliferation of information appliances and their presence in every home force builders to wire rooms for computers. The accelerated rate of technological innovation suggests that new products will continue to find their way into the marketplace and, as a consequence, into homes, and that builders will have to keep up and offer them to buyers.

Builders also have to keep abreast of emerging lifestyles and, as a result, introduce new functions in homes. Home offices, media rooms, and new kitchen technologies have all required a rapid adjustment process which is frequently imposed by trend-setting appliance manufacturers. In order to accommodate these new demands, builders have been assisted by the introduction of new building components such as wide-span, open-web joists that facilitate response to occupant needs prior to and after moving in.

The industry is also gradually embracing more prefabrication. Conventional homebuilding, with its roots in the aftermath of the Second World War, is now shifting to panelized and modular prefabricated systems. Driven by the promise of higher quality and a reduction in construction time, the factory environment, rather than the project site, offers a greater possibility for a better fit between client needs and house design. Tract developments, therefore, do not need to offer a limited number of models if the products are manufactured in a plant. Similar to processes that are currently taking place in Japan, choices made by the buyers using computers can be sent electronically from the sales office to production plants where they are constructed and delivered to the site for quick assembly.

The pronounced distinction between the building's structure and its sub-components is another change that has transformed residential construction. The share of prefinished elements in homes—those that are built in a plant and brought to the building site and "plugged in"—has increased significantly. Greater coordination between manufacturers of different subcomponents has further increased. A bathroom cabinet, for example, is now sold as a single unit incorporating a mirrored medicine cabinet, light fixture, sink, and faucet. One must recognize this trend, the final outcome of which is an opportunity for greater choice and adaptability, as the construction of future homes will be different from homes constructed previously.

Methods that simplify the participation of occupants and their choice of layouts and components have been introduced and are gaining a wide foothold in the industry. Computers have made it all possible. The ability to construct a three-dimensional image and virtually walk buyers through their as-yet-unbuilt future unit is one result of such progress.

The proliferation of television home renovation shows, handyman magazines, and how-to newspaper columns has expanded the technical knowledge and skills of average clients. As a result, buyers have become more knowledgeable and demanding when they enter a builder's sales office. They now ask

The proliferation of home decoration and renovation magazines has further educated the public about construction.

about insulating values and products, heat exchangers, and energy-efficient windows. Clients also know that eliminating a dividing wall between two rooms does not need to be overly complicated or too expensive. They therefore ask for wider choice and have greater bargaining power during the buying process.

Both builders and buyers have also benefited from the emergence of the home improvement center as an influential place in the retailing of building materials. One can find under one roof a wide range of innovative products and tools, all pointing to a great many advances ahead. Homeowners themselves have more opportunities and knowledge to participate in the modification of their homes to their own changing needs. Architects and builders can provide the physical environment for such participation to take place by introducing new building strategies such as leaving a portion of the unit's space unpartitioned for future completion by the occupants.

Small neighborhood hardware stores have been replaced by huge home improvement centers.

Homebuilding in the twenty-first century will be marked by a significant departure from present practices. The closest analogy rests within the realm of cars. Industrial design, sophisticated automated production, and response to market demand have transformed the auto industry. It is likely that the home will undergo a similar evolution. Building a house will be more like choosing and fitting prefabricated components than assembling studs.

VOLUME, ENVELOPE, AND SYSTEMS 4

A building's envelope design affects its interior layout, but for purposes of clarity in this book the home has been divided into two distinct entities. The first is the *volume, envelope, and systems*—the *macro* aspects. The second is the home's *interior space and utilities*—the *micro* aspects of a building. Within each entity, four main groups of topics have been identified. They are manipulation of volumes, spatial arrangement, growth and division, and manipulation of subcomponents. Under these four headings, several aspects, each related to the design, construction, and use of a building have been recognized. These aspects are studied and cross-checked with other relevant topics for their effect on choice and adaptability prior to and after occupancy in low-rise wood-frame housing.

Manipulation of Volumes

Urban configuration	Study of the assembly of dwellings and their effect on future change in the urban context
Unit typology	Refers to the effect that the chosen type of dwelling (e.g., rancher, bungalow, cottage) will have on adaptability
Condition of attachment	Refers to the relation that a single dwelling unit will have with an adjacent unit (e.g., detached, semidetached, row)
Ground relation	Considers the effect that the chosen placement of the building on the ground (e.g., slab on grade, basement) will have on adaptability

Spatial Arrangement

Dimensions and proportions	Considers the effect that the dimensions or the proportions of an entire dwelling or a portion of it (a floor) will have on the building's potential for adaptability
Access	Investigates how the designation of one or several accesses (e.g., front or back doors) will influence the building's present and future adaptability
Circulation	Considers the location of the circulation routes and means through a volume (e.g., vertical stair shaft)

Growth (Add-On) and Division

Growth	Refers to the incorporation of design strategies and means to enable expansion beyond the initial volume (add-on)
Division	Refers to the incorporation of design strategies and means to facilitate division of a volume (i.e., single or several levels) into smaller units, as the need arises

Manipulation of Subcomponents

Facade	Considers the effect that the building's facade will have on adaptability during construction and use. It also deals with aspects related to the occupants' ability to personalize the exterior of their home prior to or after moving in
Structure and assembly	Considers the effect that a choice of structural system (e.g., post and beam, bearing partitions) will have on the entire building's adaptability. This section also examines the building from a production-process point of view, where the entire structure can either be constructed on-site or prefabricated in a plant and delivered to the site
Services	Studies the effect that the access, type, and location of main service conduits will have on the building's adaptability

Subjects that have been considered in the study of macro issues of building design and construction that affect adaptability.

URBAN CONFIGURATION

As soon as a newly-built development is occupied, a process of change begins. This transformation process will continue throughout the life cycle of each home within the development as well as throughout the community as a whole. Changes can be as small as painting doors, replacing windows, or building a deck at the rear of a structure. But there can also be large-scale urban changes such as demolishing existing units and building infill ones in their place, or building new homes on empty lots. In the design process of a community, one can anticipate later changes on various scales and prepare for them.

Designing communities for change and adaptability has been proposed, experimented with, and attempted in the past. The intention of scholars and planners alike was to suggest an urban structure that would permit continuous modifications to compensate for unforeseen events. The theoretical backbone of these proposals was that large developments with hundreds and sometimes thousands of units would take years or even decades to complete. Thus decisions that are made at the time of conception regarding urban layout—and even the units themselves—may no longer be relevant when the time finally arrives to construct specific communities and homes. An alternative approach to the one used today, whereby a detailed master plan is prepared and approved, would be to follow a more open-ended approach. A limited number of initial major design decisions would be made as to road networks, open spaces, and the built environment. These decisions would be of a general nature and be accompanied by design guidelines that define the overall character of the proposed development. As construction proceeds, a constant process of adapting to changing market circumstances would take place. As a result of inevitable demographic, economic, life style, and technological transformations, the size, typology, cost, and stylistic expression of new units would be allowed to change to best suit the current reality.

Planning for Change of a New Community

Planning for adaptability of a new community was simulated by the author in the design of a 29-acre (11.6-hectare) site near Montreal. A conventional master plan showing roads, open spaces, and homes was first proposed. The design included an arterial road which surrounded a public open space. An alternative design approach that is more susceptible to adaptability was then suggested. It designated a central public open space and a main collector street, and it divided the site into segments. Each segment became a neighborhood unit where guidelines governing its development were enacted once development commenced. These guidelines corresponded with the overall design guidelines of the entire community. When such an open-ended process is followed, adaptability to changing circumstances on macro and micro levels would take place during the course of the community's life cycle (Friedman et al. 2001).

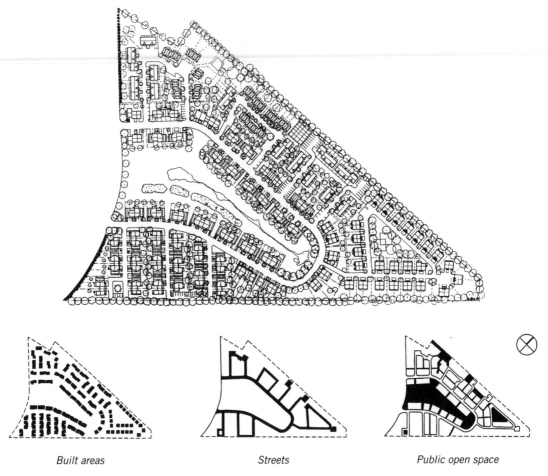

Built areas   *Streets*   *Public open space*

A detailed master plan for a 258-unit development designed in a conventional manner, with limited possibilities for future changes.

Public Green Space

The generating idea is to create a public green space around which the community will develop. The choice to center the community around a public green is an attempt to tie the developer's vision of using a public space to unite the various phases of development and thus help to foster a sense of community. Since there are limited views outward from the site, the open space serves to orientate the community inwards as well as create pleasant views for users. Finally, a series of pedestrian paths will lead users into and through the open space.

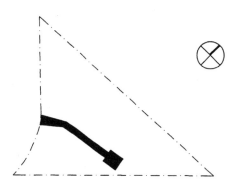

Main Collector Street

This particular collector road pattern was chosen for a number of reasons. Its overall form offers a sensitive gesture to the natural environment by contouring around the existing creek and green space. The uniform arrangement facilitates subdividing and laying out the site as well as such infrastructure components as sewage, water, and electrical grids. The limited curvilinear form of the road further ensures easy visual and physical access into and through the site by both vehicle and pedestrian traffic. The subdivision of the site into smaller blocks is an attempt to create a human scale and a diverse environment.

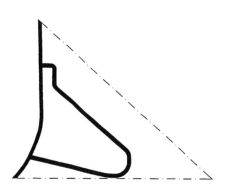

Subdivision of Development

The sizes of the subdivisions within the larger site were determined based on the developer's desire to limit the number of dwelling and commercial units that could occupy a given area. The developer felt that current market demand for the low-rise residential dwelling dictates a subdivision that could sustain approximately 80 to 100 units, a parcel of land sufficient for a first run of houses. The sequential arrangement of subdivisions was chosen for its ability to facilitate development expansion for smaller runs of dwellings while minimizing infrastructure costs.

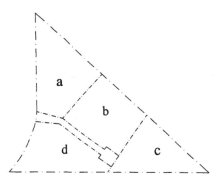

In an alternative approach, the same site has been divided into segments whose development will proceed according to changing circumstances while respecting guidelines for the entire community.

Roads

The generating idea for the neighborhood unit development is to create a semipublic greenspace that is bordered by and unites the various housing units in the subdivision. The secondary road system employed wraps around and defines the greenspace or "square" in an attempt to create an intimate and distinct community setting. The short cul-de-sac configuration of the road contributes to the developer's global vision of creating roads that make vistas and encourage walking. The juxtaposition of secondary roads to each other as well as to the collector road results in shorter, more human-scale blocks. The limited area for which each road is responsible reduces the cost of laying out such infrastructure components as sewage, water, and electrical systems.

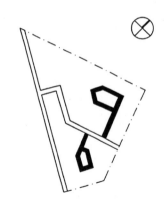

Built Form

The housing structures and patterns chosen respond to the developer's intent of building between 80 and 100 affordable low-rise housing units that cater to first-time home buyers. The construction of attached townhouses and condominium units will make the dwelling affordable while maintaining a sense of individual ownership through such features as private parking, entrances, and outdoor living areas. The layout of buildings along both the main collector and secondary roads as well as around the open space creates a strong street edge that encourages walking. The orientation of such building openings as windows and doors towards the street and open space increases safety by ensuring unobstructed visual and physical access to these spaces.

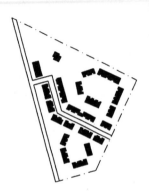

Open Space

The open space provides a distinct area that defines the neighborhood by uniting the various housing units around it and focusing public activity within it. While the semipublic space may be used by adjacent neighborhood unit developments, the intent is to provide a public forum for the users in the immediate vicinity. The use of both soft and hard surfaces to compose the semipublic open space encourages a variety of activity such as children's playgrounds, reading niches, and picnic areas. Trees are planted on portions of the site to offer shade and around the perimeter of the neighborhood to define and screen the area from adjacent neighborhoods and land uses.

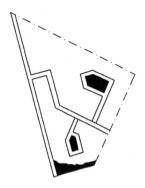

Design concept and proposed plan for the development of Plot A, one of the new community's segments.

Adapting Existing Neighborhoods

Design for adaptability can anticipate and prepare for changes on an intermediate urban scale, that of a neighborhood or a city block. Mature neighborhoods that were built decades ago frequently experience pressure to change. An aging population and increased or decreased property values place new demands on homes and their occupants or owners. In some cases, a neighborhood will see older homes demolished and replaced by new, out-of-character designs. Additions or alterations, when they do take place, often do not conform with the intentions of the original designers. However, methods have been developed for effecting a smooth introduction of changes. These involve an assessment of existing conditions, preparation of a vision for the future of the neighborhood, a design concept, a site plan, and guidelines that attempt to provide a framework for future alterations.

Such a process was simulated in an existing community, also in Montreal, where zoning bylaws had to be changed to introduce the possibility of adding an ancillary unit to the rear of properties that could serve as a dwelling or as a business. The unit could later be connected to the main structure. Some of the guidelines that would regulate the process are illustrated on the next page.

Guiding Small-Scale Interventions

Design for adaptability of urban configuration can be manifested on a smaller scale, that of building features such as windows, balconies, or roofs. As the occupancy of a community begins, smaller changes in each home will also commence. The initiators of these changes frequently run the risk of negatively altering the appearance of the building, and when many changes do occur, of transforming the character of an assembly of buildings or an entire block in a chaotic fashion.

The introduction of control measures that encourage adaptability yet define its parameters and expression in an urban setting is therefore desired. When changes take place in new infill developments in existing settings, the need to study and emulate the established community's character is paramount. Based on this assessment, guidelines for the design of new buildings and changes to existing ones will be proposed. Such a process was proposed in the Atwater dis-

Unit Subdivision:

- A rental apartment unit is permitted within the existing unit.
- Apartment unit size shall be between 300 and 500 square feet (30 and 50 square meters).

Home Offices:

- No more than $\frac{1}{3}$ of the existing unit area to a maximum of 500 square feet (50 square meters), may be used for commercial purposes within a primary unit.
- Home office uses must not interfere with the residential nature of the neighborhood and therefore should be of light commercial use.
- Acceptable uses may include home offices, child care, and professional services.
- Home office spaces are intended for the use of the residents of the home only.
- No illuminated or free-standing signs are permitted to advertise the home business; no sign may exceed 1 foot 7 in. (0.5 meter).

Ancillary Units:

- May be placed/constructed in the back yard of any existing unit.
- May not be built higher than one story or 16 feet (4.9 meters).
- Maximum unit area is 500 square feet (50 square meters).
- Shall be located within the width of the existing primary unit, and placed at least 20 feet (6 meters) from the rear facade of the existing primary unit.
- Shall be placed at least 10 feet (3 meters) from the rear property line.
- A mezzanine is permitted within the unit.
- No openings are permitted within the rear facade.
- May be attached to the primary unit using a walkway.
- Any porches, decks, or terraces:
  - shall be on the facade which faces the primary unit,
  - shall be no longer than 6 feet (1.8 meters) × 50 percent of the unit length,
  - shall be made from natural materials or simulated natural material made of recycled elements.
- Architectural Elements guidelines apply with the following change:
  - Roof material may also be wood shingles or shakes.

Example of design guidelines that regulate the process of change and adaptability of an existing community.

max. area: 500 sq. ft. (50 sq.m)

Additional apartment area as a percentage of existing unit area

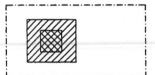

max. area: 300–500 sq. ft. (30–50 sq.m)

Home office area as a percentage of existing unit area

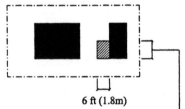

50% of the length of the unit

6 ft (1.8m)

Size and locations of porches and decks of auxiliary unit

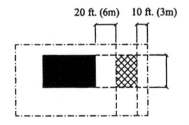

20 ft. (6m) 10 ft. (3m)

Placement of auxiliary unit

Front Addition Articulation

- No front porches are permitted.
- Balcony maximum dimension: 4 feet (1.2 meters) depth over the width of the unit; banister height shall not exceed 5 feet (1.5 meters) nor be less than 3 feet 3 inches (1 meter).
- Balconies are permitted only on the upper floors of the unit.
- Balconies shall be constructed of metal or wood.
- Balconies shall be painted in a color that complements or matches that of the other trim detailing on the unit.
- Balcony design shall be either rectangular or the combination of a rectangle and a curve.
- Landing maximum dimension: 5 feet (1.5 meters) width, 4 feet (1.2 meters) depth.
- Steps dimension: width equal to that of landing, depth no greater than 6 ft. 6 inches (2 meters).
- Alignment of additions to be centered relative to its facade opening.

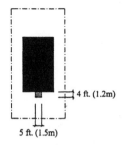
Front addition: balcony

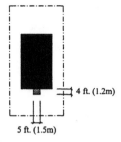
Front addition: landing

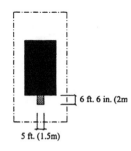
Front addition: step

Rear Addition Articulation

- Balcony maximum dimension: 10 feet (3 meters) depth over the width of the unit.
- If rear balconies are to be closed, they must conform to the standards of glazed openings of the front facade.
- Style, color and material of rear balconies should match that of the front balconies.
- Deck maximum dimension: 6 feet 6 inches (2 meters) width, 10 feet (3 meters) depth.
- Decks and terraces shall be constructed initially in pairs; one staircase shall service adjacent balconies.
- All rear additions shall be constructed of varnished wood or painted metal, in white or gray.
- Shed additions are not allowed.

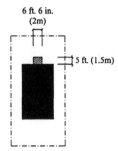
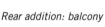
Rear addition: balcony

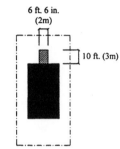
Rear addition: deck

Examples of guidelines for front and rear additions of balconies and porches to existing buildings.

trict of Montreal, where design guidelines based on the existing urban setting were devised.

The measures illustrated here ensure that when processes of change and adaptability occur at various scales—to an entire community, a section of it, or a single building feature—they will be coordinated to preserve the unique character of the community and original intentions of the designers.

UNIT TYPOLOGY

The chosen type will influence the amount of choice and adaptability in a home. In addition to determining the dwelling's appearance, the typology influences the function of the residence. The characteristics of each major type and its ability to permit adaptability are outlined in the following pages.

The Bungalow

All of the habitable rooms in a bungalow are on one level. The lower floor, a basement, contains ancillary service functions such as a laundry, mechanical services room, or a study or play space. Construction of the basement level is facilitated by the already existing need to build a foundation below the frost line [an average of 4.5 feet (1.5 meters) below ground level]. This house type is therefore more common in regions of cold climate. The basement level can be mostly below grade or extend partially above it.

The main level of the bungalow offers the possibility of open interior planning. It not only gives the impression of openness but also provides an opportunity for adaptability when proper design strategies are implemented. Bungalows are commonly built as single-family detached homes, which simplifies their expansion. However, when the lower level is expanded as well, excavation and the addition of new foundation walls make the task costly and complicated. A full addition to the bungalow is also made more difficult if the unit is located in a densely built area.

Another characteristic of the bungalow is its spread-out design. This is an advantage for adaptability since the unit perimeter allows greater choice in locating each function due to better exposure to natural light. On the other

The bungalow: The lower level can be left unfinished at first and expanded into later.

hand, it raises the cost of land and infrastructure as well as heating cost due to, among other factors, a large roof area.

The Rancher

One of the most adaptable types of dwelling is the rancher. The entire home is built on a single level above grade. This style is common in southern climatic zones where there is no freeze/thaw cycle affecting the foundation. Since all of the unit's functions are located on the same level, there are many options for open space planning and postoccupancy adaptability. Mechanical services, however, are also located on the same level, which restricts adaptability to a certain degree. Accessibility and expansion in the ranch type of dwelling are simple to execute. The roof in the rancher as built in some regions is flat, allowing for the relatively easy addition of a second floor. The perimeter and bearing walls, however, must be predesigned to support vertical expansion.

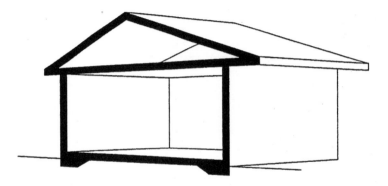

The rancher: Locating all the functions on one level permits the implementation of an open concept.

The One-and-a-Half Story

As with the bungalow, the one-and-a-half story house has a basement. In this type, however, advantage is taken of the attic for add-on expansion. The steep roof angle allows the placement of rooms on this upper floor, permitting the footprint of the house to be kept smaller than that of a bungalow. The attic space can be left unfinished at first and completion can take place as means become available. The top level, must, however, be prepared for expansion at the initial construction stage. The construction of a dormer or a skylight that can be offered as a choice during the sale by the builder will ensure natural light and ventilation. If economic concerns preclude the installation of a dormer, windows can be placed at the gable ends. This house type not only has expansion potential but also the greatest amount of floor area for the lowest capital outlay.

Since the top level does not have bearing partitions, it can be arranged in different interior configurations or be easily modified later. The space can serve as a single bedroom or be partitioned into two. Or it could become a study or a hobby room at first and then be turned into a bedroom. The vertical configuration of the one-and-a-half story also has an energy efficiency advantage. The upper floor benefits from the heat that rises from below. It is common to see a fan at the top of the stairs to circulate the warm air.

The one-and-a-half story: This style allows expansion into the attic.

The one-and-a-half story dwelling was very popular during the post–World War II construction boom. The economic advantage of the design as well as its suitability for young families made it a prime choice by builders and buyers. With time, zoning regulations started to limit the design in favor of larger homes. This type can be found today in many old neighborhoods, and an examination of its interior demonstrates remarkable versatility. Nonetheless, several of its design and construction principles can be found in newer homes as well.

The Two-Story

When more than two bedrooms are needed on the upper floor, the two-story house is a suitable prototype. This unit type is often used as part of a row when the lots are narrow. One of the advantages of this design is its versatility as to the use of the floors. The two-story house can easily become a three-story when the basement level is introduced as a living area. When the basement windows are

The two-story: When an appropriate structural system is selected, the second floor
permits a variety of bedroom configurations.

placed well above grade, sufficient natural light will be let in. As such, each of
the levels, with an appropriate area, can be designed to become an independent dwelling unit either at the pre- or postoccupancy stages. Special attention
must then be paid to access to and circulation through the structure (see section on Access and Circulation).

Based on height restrictions in different locations, the roof can be made
steeper to become an attic, allowing for an add-in expansion possibility. When the
two-story house is built as a detached home with an attached garage, expansion
from the second floor to the top of the garage can take place. The garage therefore
needs to have a structurally sound flat roof aligned with the second level's floor.
The circulation on this floor also needs to accommodate future expansion in order
to avoid the inconvenience of routing a passageway through a room.

The Split-Level

This house type is a hybrid between the bungalow and the rancher, and it
enjoys the advantages of both. The split-level home was developed to protect

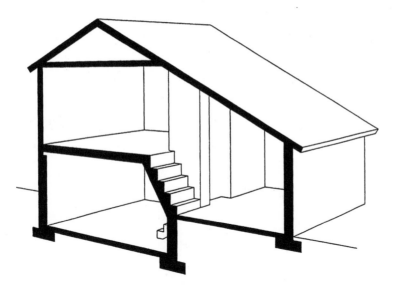

Split-level: The lower level of this style can become an independent
unit prior to or following occupancy.

the foundation from the freeze/thaw cycle and at the same time allow a portion
of it to be at grade. It is common to see a parking garage occupying the front
end of the street-level portion of the house. When the occupants are in need of
additional space, the garage can be converted into a living space or even
become an independent dwelling. This change necessitates alternative parking
arrangements, however.

Since the unit is designed on different levels, it is possible to arrange the
spaces within it according to different zones and functions. It is also an
advantage when the possibility of dividing the structure into smaller units is
considered. Each level could become an independent dwelling with its own
entry.

Other attributes of these dwelling types as they affect adaptability will be
illustrated in the sections that follow.

CONDITION OF ATTACHMENT

The majority of dwellings in North America are single-family detached homes. Others are semidetached (attached to another unit on one side) and row housing, where the homes, with the exception of the end units, are attached on both sides. Accommodating buyers' space needs at the preoccupancy stage as well as adaptability during residency will be affected by the condition of attachment.

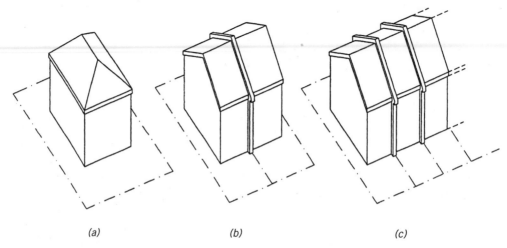

(a)   (b)   (c)

Alternative conditions of dwellings' attachment: (a) detached, (b) semidetached, and (c) row housing.

Altering Urban Forms

The choice of dwelling typology and its condition of attachment affect urban configuration and its potential for change. Detached homes due to their limited number of physical restrictions, most readily undergo alteration and expansion as urban assembly. Most expansions take place in the rear of the unit. When the home is properly set back, the possibility exists of adding to the front in the form of building or enclosing a porch. The process of growth

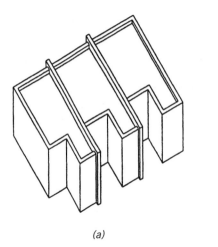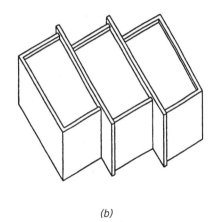

(a)

(b)

Preparation for rear expansion of row housing: (a) creating a back alcove, and (b) staggering row housing.

in row housing, on the other hand, is slower since it is uncommon to expand a single unit in a block without influencing the character of the row. However, initial design strategies can be devised whereby subsequent expansion will be less noticeable throughout the entire configuration. Staggering units or creating an exterior alcove that can be filled at a later stage are two possible strategies.

Aligning Floor Levels

The adaptability of the chosen unit's typology will also be affected by the condition of attachment. During construction of multistory dwellings built in a row, when the builder wants to offer the choice of combining small units horizontally, it will be easier to expand when the floor levels are aligned. In a split-level detached home, the different levels allow the division of a single-family home into several units, where each level could become an independent dwelling with its own access.

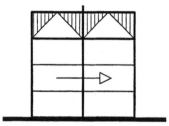
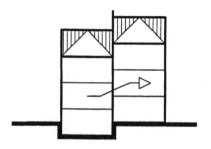

Alignment of floors simplifies horizontal expansion   *Difference of level will create a circulation challenge*

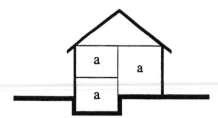
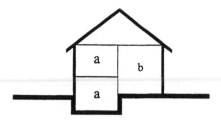

*Due to its configuration, a split-level home (left) provides an easier way of turning
a single-family unit into a multi-family unit*

Alignment of row housing levels (top) and the possibility of turning a single-family, split-level home into several units (bottom).

The Square Footprint

A unit with wider proportions will commonly be more prone to adaptability. As a result of having a larger facade area, the flexibility of introducing natural light to more rooms increases. A home with square proportions, detached or

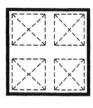
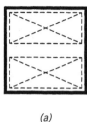
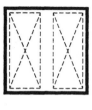
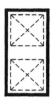

(a)   (b)

Comparisons of square footprints (a) with a narrow one (b) with relation to interior adaptability. A square footprint has more adaptability options.

part of a row, will also permit a greater choice of interior configurations. In the upper floors of a narrow row house [narrower than 16 feet (5 meters)], one bedroom only can be placed at either end, whereas in a wider unit more rooms can be located at the edges. A wider lot, however, will incur a higher cost of land and infrastructure.

Placing an Entry Door

The condition of attachment influences the location of access to a unit. Whether focusing on a main access or a back door, initial design strategies need to consider future alteration to the dwelling. In a detached home, the access can be placed along any of the four perimeter walls, whereas in a semi-detached home, the placement is reduced to three walls, and to two walls for access in a row house. Thus the move from a single detached dwelling to a row house diminishes the range of adaptability as far as access is concerned.

A detached or semidetached unit can be designed for the introduction of future doors. In a well-marked place, where the studs have been spaced accordingly and a lintel installed, a door can be inserted at a later stage to permit the division of a single home into two dwelling units. Another possibility is to place a window in the wall, which can later be turned into a door.

In row housing, when the width permits, the placement of the main entry door close to the common wall provides an opportunity to subsequently build another entry. This will allow the division of a single-family unit into a multi-family configuration or the creation of an independent space, such as a home office or rental unit, with its own access. The end unit of a row will be more

  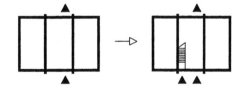

Initial accesses   *A second door allows the division of detached home*   *Preparation for the introduction of another door in a row house permits the conversion of a single into a multifamily unit*

Location of accesses in a detached unit and in a row.

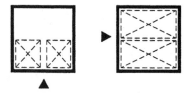

Optional placement of access in
a detached home.

adaptable since it has exposure to natural light on three sides. This adaptability can be increased further when the main door is located on the side elevation, leaving both front and back spaces free for manipulation.

The exact placement of the access in the building's facade will significantly affect its potential for adaptability. Although placing the door in the center of the front wall is a common configuration, this limits the potential for future division of the space. The preferred condition would be to locate the access along the lateral wall in the cases of single detached homes, semidetached dwellings, and row houses.

Attachment, Growth, and Division

A dwelling's condition of attachment will affect its potential for growth and division. The extent of the growth could be the addition of a large volume, such as an adjacent dwelling, or the building of a bay window that extends beyond the building's perimeter. The process can also be reversed, and a large home could be divided into several units. The degree of expansion or division depends, among other factors, on the lot size and on zoning regulations, including allowances for setback and land coverage. The detached home will present fewer constraints for expansion, whereas semidetached and row housing provide less freedom for growth beyond the original shell.

The possibility of annexing adjacent space in a multistory attached arrangement (semidetached or row house) is another variation on expansion of volume. In order for such possibilities to occur, the layout of the units needs to be planned at the outset and a place designated for the introduction of a passage between spaces. Allowing for the joining of units during the design phase can

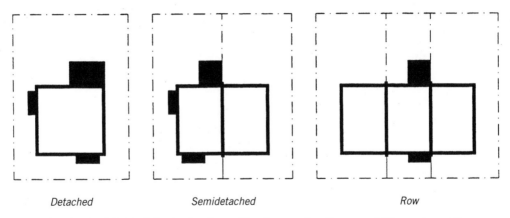

Detached *Semidetached* *Row*

Expansion beyond the building's structure either by constructing an addition or by adding a bay window.

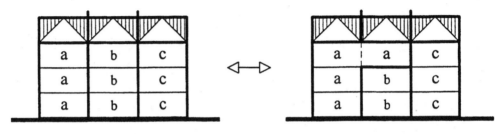

Original configuration *Unit a expanded horizontally to annex the top floor of unit b*

Expansion and division of adjacent spaces in a multistory attached structure.

provide the builder with an opportunity to offer a variety of unit sizes within the same building assembly. This would allow a welcome mix of household types and incomes.

One Versus Two Windows

The condition of attachment affects exposure to natural light and ventilation, which are key features when adaptability is sought. The freedom to place functions along the facades is obviously more limited in semidetached units or row

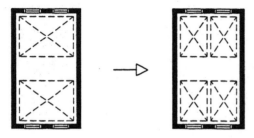

The installation in a row house of two windows rather than one will facilitate the division of one large space into two, when the width permits.

housing. The condition in both situations will improve as the building width increases, yet their cost is also likely to increase due to the higher cost of a larger plot of land. The minimum width that permits the division of a facade in a row is 18 feet (5.5 meters), to allow for the creation of two rooms measuring 9 feet (2.8 meters) each—a minimum suitable width for a room. The design of a single window in row housing will also limit future division of a large space into two rooms, and vice versa. The installation of two smaller windows would be preferable.

Framing for Future Stairs

The selected structural system will influence the degree of choice and adaptability in various conditions of attachment. In a detached home, the introduction of bearing partitions will limit internal adaptability. The situation is more critical in an attached condition. The introduction of row housing is frequently made to save costly land through increased density; therefore the units have limited width. The width can commonly vary between 12 and 25 feet (3.7 and 7.6 meters) without having to introduce bearing partitions, and as a result, internal changes will be easier to introduce either prior to or following occupancy.

A more challenging aspect is the introduction of stairs to an upstairs level after the unit has been constructed. The building of stairs perpendicular to the joists will be costly when the direction of the joists is from wall to wall. Perhaps

 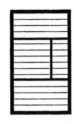 

Framed floor   Preparing appropriate beams and joists   Placing stairs following removal of part of the joists

Framing a floor for the future introduction of stairs.

the most desirable solution is to frame the floor in advance in such a way as to facilitate the future introduction of stairs.

Connection to Main Services

The placement of a building's access to the main service feeders such as a drain or water main will be influenced by its condition of attachment and will have implications for future adaptability. Whereas the designers, builders, and occupants of detached homes will enjoy minimal limitations, the situation requires

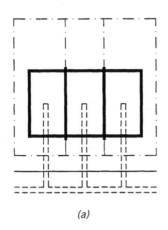

(a)

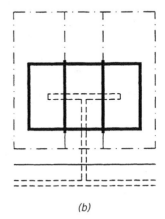

(b)

Possible connections of services' access to the main; a single-entry arrangement as in (b) will be less expensive to install than multiple-entry connections as in (a), but its future adaptability will be limited.

more attention in the case of a semidetached dwelling or row house. When a row is proposed in a condominium arrangement where all of the occupants of the dwellings own the entire structure in common, a single entry of services can be designed, thereby saving on expenses associated with connection to each unit. This arrangement limits adaptability, however, since the occupants rely on a single entry. In addition, a preferred place for the wet functions in the home could be next to common walls, allowing easy connection to water supply and drains.

GROUND RELATION

Several options are available to the designer regarding the position of the home on the ground. The options will be affected by zoning regulations, desired urban configuration, and budget. The choices are to place the building at ground level; to place the lower level (basement) either fully or partially underground; or to have a split-level whereby one portion of the structure would be below grade and the other portion above grade. Each choice will influence several factors affecting adaptability.

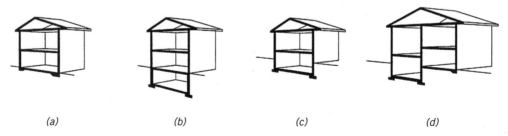

| (a) | (b) | (c) | (d) |

Ground relation of dwelling units alternatives: (a) on grade, (b) below grade, (c) partially below grade, and (d) split level.

Homes with an Underground Level

Units with an underground level possess the advantage of having a "bonus area" in the form of a basement. The basement can house the family's utility functions such as mechanical or laundry rooms, or more common spaces like a family room or a study. This underground space, however, has its own limitations, primarily in the limited degree of access to natural light, susceptivity to

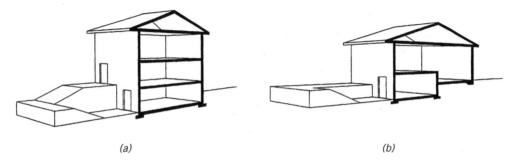

Independent unit in the basement of a multistory structure (a) and a split-level dwelling (b). When independent access is provided in advance, the basement level can readily become an independent unit.

dampness, and problems with ventilation. Yet basement levels can become and in many cases are used as spaces for an independent dwelling unit or even a business with its own entrances and civic number. Attention must therefore be paid to the design of direct access from the outside. In a split-level home, conditions of adaptability are simpler because there are more opportunities for exposure to light and ventilation. The on-ground portion of the house can also be converted to an independent dwelling. If the accessory unit is in the under-ground portion of a split-level home, a ramp would have to be built if it is to be used by a senior. Expansion beyond the original perimeter of the home with a basement poses a challenge. The process requires excavation, which is often costly and an inconvenience when an existing home is located in a densely-built area.

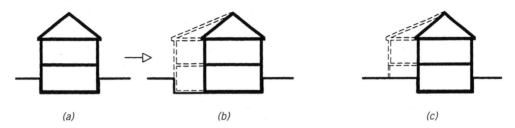

(a)   (b)   (c)

Preparing for expansion in a unit with an underground level (a). When there is an under-ground level, expansion of the upper floors requires the extension of the foundation (b) or the use of support columns (c).

Increasing exposure to natural light in the underground level of an existing home is a difficult task. Cutting openings in a foundation wall is an inconvenient and costly undertaking. The result is a limited number of interior adaptability options and the need to install more light fixtures. When possible, a retaining wall can be constructed at a distance from the back of the house. A door can be placed at the rear wall, creating a below-grade patio. When a glass door is installed, it can also let in natural light.

DIMENSIONS AND PROPORTIONS

When the dimensions and the proportions of a home or a single floor within it are considered with respect to their influence on choice and adaptability, several factors need to be studied. They are all related to the design configuration that will yield the greatest number of variations of the entire structure or the spaces within it. Additionally, the building's proportions will affect its appearance.

Versatile Homes

The common tendency in the planning of new tract developments is to repeat the same dwelling type and design. In addition, as a result of stringent zon-

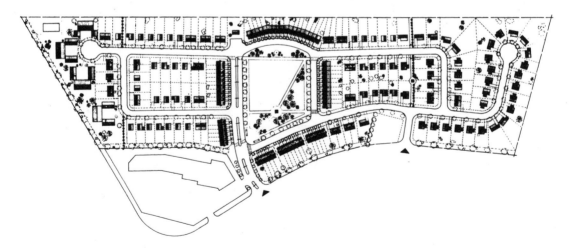

A planned-unit development (PUD) showing a range of unit types within the same project.

ing regulations, very little choice and diversity of configurations are offered within the same project, leading to demographic and economic similarity of buyers.

With proper consideration of the dwelling type and its proportions, the same building can be built as a single-family detached structure, semidetached home, or a row house. Approximate proportions would be a width of 20 feet (6.1 meters) and a height of 35 feet (10.7 meters), including the roof. In a large development, the units could then be arranged in a variety of configurations according to the desired urban character of the community, and a greater number of choices could be offered.

Front or Side Main Entrances

One of the aspects that must be considered early in the design of a single-family detached home is the functional and the spatial configuration of the home's front elevation. When the entry door is located in the middle of the front facade, the interior space will naturally be divided into two areas with circulation in between. This configuration limits adaptability. When the design permits the location of a door near one of the side walls, it provides greater exposure to natural light and circulation to the upstairs level in the event of the structure being divided. Another strategy is to propose a side entrance which frees the front elevation from access and circulation and provides greater opportunity for division of that space from the rest of the unit.

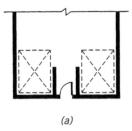
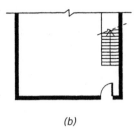
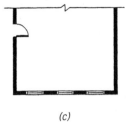

(a) (b) (c)

Three options for the location of an entry door—(a), middle entrance, which divides the front space into two; (b), entrance adjacent to a side wall, which allows greater flexibility as well as access to an upper level; and (c), side entrance, which provides greater opportunities for division in the front space.

Easy Conversion

When a multistory structure is conceived and sold as a dwelling that can serve either a single family or several families, the area of each floor must be sufficient to become a self-contained, independent dwelling. Therefore, each level needs to be designed and spaced to accommodate all of the basic functions. The maximum size of the floor will depend, of course, on the client's means and the minimum size on its desired liveability. A 500-square-foot (50-square-meter) floor area can become a bachelor unit, whereas an 800-square-foot (80-square-meter) unit would be sufficient for two bedrooms.

ACCESS AND CIRCULATION

The placement of a main or secondary entrance to a home affects its internal circulation. Since one must reach the various functions of the unit from the main door, the access will have a pivotal role on how the space is designed. It also affects choice and adaptability. Whereas circulation in the interior of a dwelling will be investigated later, this section considers the effect on the overall spatial arrangements of a structure.

Entrances to Single- or Multifamily Homes

In a single-family detached home, there is greater flexibility in locating the entrance. In fact, any of the perimeter walls can accommodate a door. In a multistory, multifamily dwelling, the placement of an access that must serve several dwelling units has even greater importance, since it can influence the spatial configuration of the entire structure. More important as far as adaptability is concerned, is how changes in the structure, such as between units, can take place: how a structure that was designed to accommodate three households, for example, could become a home for two households or even a single one, and vice versa. A ground-floor unit could also accommodate an office or an apartment for a member of an extended family.

Locating the main entrance along one of the lateral walls frees the front elevation for windows and allows exposure to natural light. If the structure is part of a row, the end wall will also provide structural support for the installation of

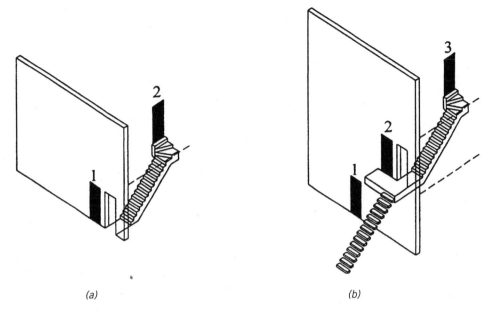

Each dwelling unit has its own entry door and stairs (a); common stairs serve the upper two dwellings in a triplex (b).

stairs. When two or three dwelling units are built within a structure, each unit occupying a floor, there are several strategies to arranging the access. The first is to provide each dwelling with direct access from the outside. Each unit would have its own stairs. The second strategy is to design a staircase shared by all, which would yield a greater adaptability since only relatively small changes would have to be made in order to change the structural configuration from a single-family to a two- or three-family structure.

Stair Configuration

When a common stair shaft is used by all the units in a multistory dwelling, its configuration and the enclosure around it will be the main tools for effecting adaptability. These aspects will have a bearing on the ability to join units on different floors when needed.

Stair systems include straight runs, landings, and winders that can be combined and arranged according to the desired composition of the units in the structure. The circumstances that bring about the need to manipulate the stairs

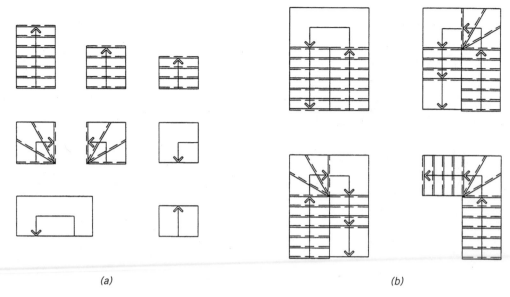

(a)

(b)

Stair subcomponents (a) and a variety of assemblies (b).

can be the offering of a choice to buyers during construction or a postoccupancy rearrangement.

Stair components extend the opportunity of introducing intermediate floors (mezzanines) in a structure with tall stories. They also allow the division of a volume into a range of configurations either before or after occupancy. A lower floor, for example, can become an office or a rental unit with its own entry. Other stairs can also be installed within the home in addition to the main ones. The structural preparation for additional stairs following occupancy was previously outlined.

Construction of stairs in a wood-frame structure is often considered time-consuming and complicated. The stairs are built on-site and their riser dimension is usually calculated according to the difference in height between floors. Several innovations have been introduced in recent years, all based on viewing the stair structure as a set of prefabricated subcomponents that can be assembled and adjusted on-site as well as later in the life of the structure. One of these systems is detailed on page 97.

The ability to alter the building configuration from a single unit to a duplex or triplex depends on the enclosure around the stair shaft. In a single-family

Since it takes a long time to build conventional stairs on-site in a wood-frame house, as well as being costly and inflexible, an adjustable modular steel staircase framing system was developed. It is a kit that can be assembled for any measurement and staircase configuration, and is designed for quick and easy on-site installation. Consisting of two lightweight steel components—the first is a step support and the other a stringer—it also includes a dozen connectors. All the steps and risers can be installed by a twist of the prefixed pegs. For use during the construction phase, reusable steps are included which can be easily disconnected when the proper finishing is to be installed.

The free-standing staircase is installed right after the wall studs have been built and it can be easily screwed onto the studs. The system can also be easily attached to concrete surfaces and fitted with steel treads and risers. The adjustable modular steel frame stays up permanently, while its sturdy temporary steel steps can be unbolted when the builder is ready to put in the finished steps. If the staircase needs to be covered, the system is fitted with permanent weatherproof treads and risers. Riser heights and step widths are equally distributed and therefore installation costs of the prefabricated steps and risers are low.

All of the components of the system are welded together by the injection of liquid polyester resin, forming units resistant to squeaking and vibration. The stringers are reinforced with fiberglass and made of engineered wood oriented–strand board. In addition, all installations include an underside wooden framing onto which drywall or a wood finish can be screwed.

(a)   *(b)*

Conventional wood stairs (a) and prefabricated stairs made by Stairframe™ (b).

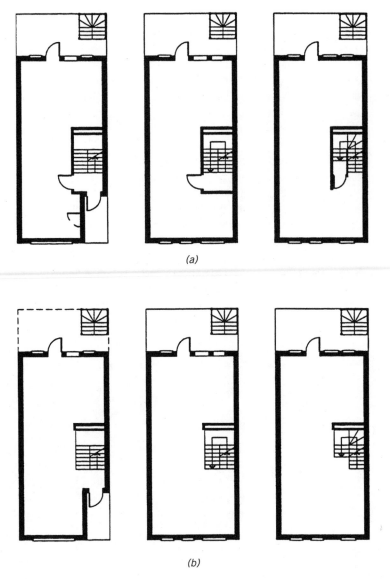

(a)

(b)

Different enclosures around the same stair configuration for a triplex
(a) and for a single-family home (b).

home, for example, since all the floors are used by the same household, no enclosure is necessary. When the building is used by three families, an enclosure and entry door are needed on each floor. Since this arrangement might change and some of the enclosure later be demolished, it is preferable, when possible, to avoid the installation of utility conduits in these walls.

GROWTH (ADD-ON) AND DIVISION OF VOLUMES

The urban appearance of old towns and villages is largely a result of constant expansion beyond the perimeter of the house and the change of its dwellings. Whether it is due to a need for additional space or as an economic strategy of starting small and expanding later as means become available, growth has taken a variety of forms. Dividing large spaces into smaller ones is also common, although less documented. Design strategy that permits growth or division of volumes must respect numerous parameters. These encompass fundamental elements of design, such as circulation, services, materials, light, and ventilation, which can impair the process if the original design is insensitive to such aspects.

How to Grow

Growth of a building is manifested in a variety of forms. The chosen method of expansion depends on the conditions under which the initial structure was conceived. The most common expression of growth is a rear addition where a new structure is built and integrates with an existing building. Expansion can also take the form of adding a new floor to an existing house, which is common in homes with flat roofs. In the case of a pitched roof, trusses or rafters can be removed, a floor constructed, and the roof rebuilt. It is possible to have a downward addition. Although not very common in North America, the addition takes place when the home is constructed on pillars, leaving open space underneath that can subsequently be enclosed.

Addition can also occur as a bridge between two existing buildings. The expansion would see the construction of a segment that occupies the space

Adding a floor to a house

Adding a rear extension to an existing house

Adding a second floor to an existing structure (e.g., building on top of a garage)

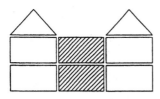

Bridging between two buildings

Connecting an ancillary unit to the main house

Adding a component (e.g., a bay window)

Expressions of growth of dwelling units.

between them. Constructing an independent ancillary unit and connecting it to the main structure at a later stage is another form of growth. Such a process must conform with local zoning regulations (many municipalities prohibit the building of such structures). Another simple addition is to add to a building a marginal space in the form of a component. Replacing a regular window with a bay, for example, will add only a small amount of space, yet it can make a room seem significantly larger.

The chosen unit typology, whether a bungalow, single- or multistory structure, or split-level dwelling unit, will have advantages and disadvantages when growth or division of spaces is considered. In general, when the expansion is at ground level, there will be fewer complications than when an addition includes a basement and an upper-floor unit. The designer needs initially to arrange the interior layout in such a way that extensive renovation will not be needed once a decision to expand is made.

Access to the Addition

Paying attention to access and circulation while designing a unit for expansion prevents a situation where a passageway to the added portion would have to be through a room. A central, double-loaded corridor that acts as a spine will facilitate expansion and not be blocked by an addition. This type of layout is suitable for a detached home where natural light can penetrate from side elevations. On the other hand, the solution is not effective in the case of an attached condition without exposure to natural light. A similar design strategy was used by Rabaneck et al. in their proposal for an adaptable home (Rabeneck 1974a).

In a row house situation, exposure to natural light is available only from the front and rear. It is common in low-income housing, primarily in the developing world, to build around a court which in addition to providing light serves as outdoor private space and helps with cross-ventilation.

When an expanded section is designed to become an independent dwelling unit, considerations of entries and exits for both units are necessary. In most municipalities, every dwelling is required to have two access ways for safety reasons. A similar consideration would be applied when a large unit is subdivided.

A central, double-loaded corridor will prevent the need to pass through a room once an addition is built, in a proposal by Rabaneck et al. for an adaptable home.

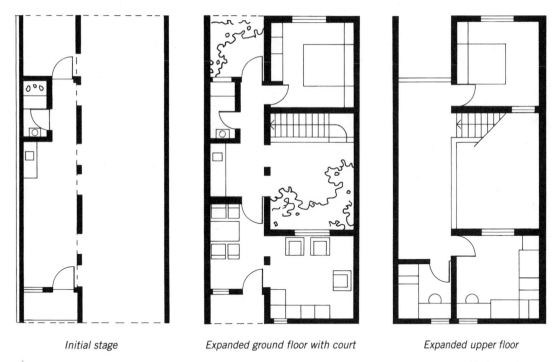

Initial stage   *Expanded ground floor with court*   *Expanded upper floor*

In this expandable, low-cost row house design, a court was introduced to provide natural light and cross-ventilation.

Expanding in Dense Neighborhoods

An addition to an existing house which is built in a densely populated area is a logistically complex task. Access by and use of heavy machinery in a rear expansion is often a challenge. Therefore consideration must be made to prepare for such an expansion structurally or, alternatively, to employ prefabricated systems.

When conventional construction is used, the new section can be structurally independent or it can use the existing structure as part of its support. In the former case, a prefabricated system can be employed. The addition could be made of a factory-built model that would be brought to the site and placed on a perimeter foundation wall or piers. A well-documented addition of this nature, although not common in North America, is the "granny flat," an independent structure to house an aging member of the family. The use of panelized systems will also simplify and shorten construction time. Once again, a foundation must be prepared to support the wall panels and the roof. When the expansion uses the existing house as part of its structure, beams or columns need to be affixed to it.

Locating Wet Functions

The connection of the added portion to the existing one will also consider the placement of utilities. During the design of a unit for addition, wet functions such as the bathroom and kitchen can be placed in the rear. When the expansion takes place, these rooms will be centrally located in the combined structure.

Dividing an Expanded Home

The reason for expanding a home might be the need for more space for a growing family. Yet in the later part of the life cycle, the process is reversed, and the household size decreases when grown-up children leave home to form their own households. This decline in space needs can lead to a portion of the house tak-

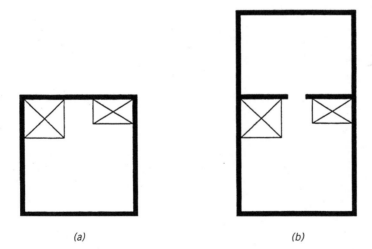

(a)   (b)

Placing wet functions in the rear of a structure (a) will facilitate access to utilities when an addition is built (b).

ing on other uses. The newly available space can become a hobby room, a suite for a guest, or can even be divided from the house to form an independent dwelling unit. The unit can be rented out to compensate for a decline in income in a home with retired occupants.

Several measures ought to be taken in order to facilitate such a process. Direct access from the outside to the unit is a prime consideration. A passageway along the side of the house to the back needs to be arranged. Conversion of the back exit door to an entry door can also take place, as well as preparation of the plumbing for the installation of a new kitchen and bathroom when one does not exist. In a multistory dwelling, the introduction of new stairs will have to be made, with the preparation of floor joists for such an eventuality.

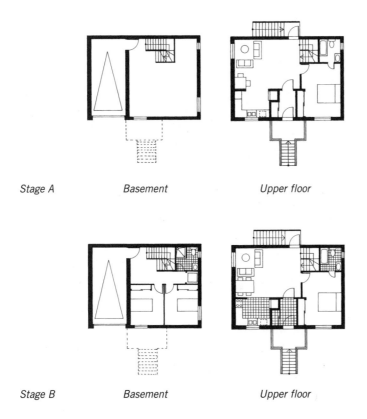

Stage A   Basement   Upper floor

Stage B   Basement   Upper floor

In this expandable home, the back portion of the dwelling was converted by the owners into an independent rental unit to compensate for a decline in family income.

Stage C   Basement   Upper floor

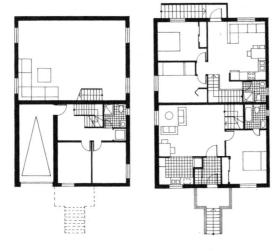

Stage D   Basement   Upper floor

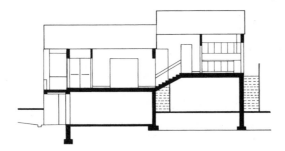

(Continued)   *Section through an expanded home*

FACADE

Once homes are constructed, it is hard to change their facades. Inserting a new window or door is labor-intensive and costly. Since the building envelope and the floor are structurally integrated, changes to the facade often require structural intervention as well. A lintel, beam, or column might have to be introduced to support the upper floor. It is therefore preferable to envision such possible future changes and prepare for them during the initial design stage. Moreover, changes to the exterior would likely be the result of changes to the interior; as a result, it is necessary to view the entire building as an integrated entity.

Since the building's exterior also reflects an image that a homeowner wants to project to the street, the desire is often to personalize the facade. In custom-designed homes, the clients usually participate in determining the exterior styles and articulations. It is more challenging to personalize a facade in a tract development when the future occupants' identities are unknown, and in particular in a row house where the units are identical. This section will deal with these concerns in the process of preparing a building for choice and adaptability of the building envelope.

Harmony and Diversity

Detached homes can be built without any stylistic relation to neighboring units. In most cases, however, they form part of a development of such homes. The tendency is to offer to buyers several choices of elevation designs that suit a variety of interior configurations. Designers often try to create linguistic harmony between the offered designs in order to provide some sense of visual similarity between the units. The case is quite different in developments of semidetached or row housing where the units are attached. Facades of housing developments where identical units are built are often repeated for economic reasons. Using windows of the same size and style could get a builder a volume discount from his framing team and manufacturer. The effect of such a streetscape, primarily one with row housing, is frequently unpleasant and sterile.

The study of traditional row housing developments in many North American urban centers suggests that personalization was attempted by builders of earlier

(a)

(b)

New row housing developments are often repetitive and sterile, creating unpleasant environments (a), whereas in older projects the facades are articulated and choice was offered to occupants (b).

communities. Variety and choice were provided, and a range of articulations created diversity within harmony. Personalization usually also happens by accretion. Over time, occupants add their personal touches to the exterior of a unit. Painting a hand railing, entry door, or window sill, and putting out flower boxes distinguish one home from another in a row. Despite the fact that such a process may be intuitive, the facade can be designed and prepared for occupant intervention.

The study of contemporary building practices shows that when carpentry contractors are aware prior to the construction of the frame, they often do not mind alterations in facade openings as long as the variations are not radically different from one another. With regard to the opening sizes and to the windows themselves, small numbers can be selected and alternated within the composition. The challenge, therefore, is to propose a methodology that simplifies both personalization at the time of conception and construction and adaptability during use.

The three basic formal strategies for the location and treatment of windows (the essential component in the articulation of residential facades) are: *systematic repetition, random order,* and *composition.* The strategy of systematic repetition accommodates the concept of adaptability by allowing the application of a universal standard of window placement which could accept any function behind it, but such a strategy eliminates the potential for personal identity and must therefore be considered unsuitable. The second option of random place-

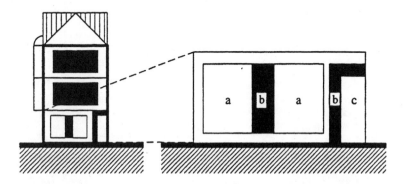

Opening zone in the lower floor of a facade showing: (a) infill areas in which windows will be installed, and (b) opaque areas representing walls.

ment of windows based on occupant preferences and plan considerations accommodates a high degree of individual identity but runs the risk of undermining the reading of a single module as a unified whole. The result of absolute random placement of windows would be visual chaos. Some vertical emphasis is required to carry the eye upward and indicate the importance of the single unit over the row.

While compositional concerns impose some measure of constraint on the sizing and placement of windows, they impart a sense of stability and recognition to the facade. The element of personalization in the placement and specific sizing of windows reduces adaptability in the long term, in the sense that interior modifications could also lead to changes in the facade. While this aspect may be considered as an obstacle to adaptability, the appropriate choice of facade materials, such as stucco, makes such facade changes relatively easy. Certain code restrictions, such as limiting the sill height to a minimum of three feet (one meter), also facilitate future interior changes.

A methodology that promotes choice and adaptability is one that is made up of two principal elements: *opening zones* and *infill components.* The opening zones are areas in the facade in which infill components can be placed. Infill com-

Facade arrangements where choice was offered to the occupants within a prearranged framework of opening zones.

ponents are windows and doors which fill part of the opening zone. The rest is constructed similar to the rest of the facade. The opening zone is structurally prepared for the future introduction and change of windows. The introduction of a new opening in the zone will therefore not require a major structural intervention.

A menu of facade options can be prepared for future occupants by the designer and offered by the builder. The offered items and their proportions will permit the personalization of a dwelling unit within a desired coherence and harmony.

Effect of Expansion on the Facade

When a building is expanded, a fundamental consideration is the effect on the facade. Two main issues are to be examined. The first is functional: whether the addition will fit with the functioning of the old part. Concerns regarding blocking natural light, access, circulation, and ventilation must be studied. The second aspect has to do with the appearance of the building. Consideration must be given to whether the addition affects the exterior character of the home.

With regard to functional aspects, the placement of windows in the initial design requires foresight. Whereas there is little concern about light and ventilation in a detached home, the challenge is greater in an attached situation.

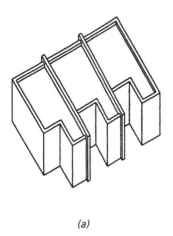
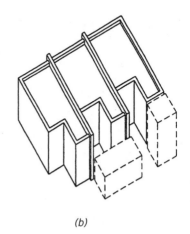

(a)   (b)

Row housing (a) can be designed so that future rear additions do not block natural light, ventilation, or access (b).

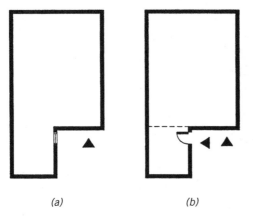

(a)   *(b)*

A long side window (a) could become the door for a home office on the lower level, enabling visitors to enter directly without entering the unit first (b).

In this expanded home the added right portion was designed to blend in with the older section.

This can be addressed by proposing a building configuration that preserves a light well once the expansion has been made. The area can remain open or the roof can be glazed to create an interior atrium.

When a single-family, multistory dwelling is designed—one which at the construction stage could be sold as a multifamily house or transformed into one—the architect can propose additional doors to allow easy access to each floor. In addition, if a lower floor could house a different function, such as a home office, a long side window could easily be turned into a door.

The overall appearance of a building will also need to be considered. Design strategies can follow the style of the original building or ignore it. Most towns with established zoning regulations often demand that the addition adhere to the existing design, respecting proportions, dimensions, and materials. An initial design that anticipates expansion can accommodate such a process by not using hard-to-find, trendy materials that will be difficult to procure later, when the expansion is constructed. Good expansions are frequently unnoticeable and blend in well with the initial section.

When the slope of a pitched roof permits, an internal expansion to the attic, which was left unfinished initially, can be planned in advance. A dormer window or a skylight can be constructed initially since its later addition would be difficult and costly to introduce.

STRUCTURE AND ASSEMBLY

The decision as to the choice of structural system and its design will greatly influence the level of adaptability in a home. Several possibilities are available to the designer of a wood-frame structure, including the use of a post-and-beam system where the walls (either exterior or interior) act as infill components. Another approach would be to build a framing assembly either as a balloon or a platform frame. The balloon frame, where the studs are continuous from the foundation to the roof, is rarely used today. In a platform frame, the floor is built first and then the rest of the structural system is constructed on top of it. In general, since the floor and the envelope are an integrated system, major structural changes to the facade require the support of the floor above and, as such, limited adaptability is possible (see Facade section). Other factors that are likely to influence adaptability either at the pre- or postoccupancy stages are the presence of interior load-bearing walls and the type of floor joists used.

Conventional Floor System

In a conventional floor system, floor joists are made of dimensional lumber. They are usually 2 inches (50 mm) thick and either 6, 8, 10, or 12 inches (150, 200, 250 or 300 mm) wide, depending on the loading conditions, length of span, spacing between the joists, type and grade of lumber, and amount of deflection allowed according to the building code. The length of dimensional lumber joists depends on their section's size, but the average span ranges between 8 feet, 7 inches and 21.5 feet (2.7 and 6.6 meters). Joists made of dimensional lumber longer than 15 feet (4.6 meters) are not standard and therefore are costly. When the house dimensions exceed the length of conventional-length joists, the joists must rest on bearing partitions or on beams.

Since bearing partitions are an integral part of the structure, they cannot be moved easily, and as a result they restrict interior changes. Introducing an opening or removing the partition altogether requires strengthening the wall in order to maintain the building's structural integrity. When the design of a home is prepared for future adaptability, and a conventional floor system is used, certain considerations are essential. The designer can, for example, place the bearing partitions around functions or areas where the possibility of needed changes is low. The moving of a bathroom, for instance, is often costly and rarely attempted, the same as for the walls which enclose stairs. These partitions can be bearing walls in a conventional structure.

Engineered Floor Systems

In recent years, alternative floor-joist systems have been developed. The systems have considerably improved the current method of construction with regard to adaptability. The thrust of these products is their ability to increase the span as well as to use less wood. The key feature of these engineered floor systems is a web that comes in different forms. In one such product, the wooden I-joist, the web is made of laminated veneer lumber (LVL) flanges or oriented strand board (OSB) webs which are more resistant to water damage.

(a)   (b)

Conventional floor joists made of dimensional lumber (a) and alternative open-web floor trusses (b).

An additional product is the metal-web space joist made of high-tension galvanized steel plates connected to top and bottom wood flanges (usually studs). The metal plates are pressed into the side of the top and bottom wood sections. Metal-web space joists are light and can be installed by the framing crew. They can span up to 40 feet (12.2 meters) without intermediate support. Another advantage is the ability to use them in floor, roof, or even wall construction when a thicker envelope is needed. Another product that permits greater adaptability is the open-web wood joist, where the web is made of glued wood sections. With this product, which is used in both light and heavy construction, the web components are finger-jointed using special glue.

The contribution that these products have made is in freeing the interior space from bearing partitions and in allowing the building envelope and floors to be made independent of the interior partitions. Another significant contribution of these products resides in simplifying the passage of utility conduits. The open web eliminates the need to drill through it and to weaken it as a result, allowing greater ease and flexibility in locating wet functions on the floor.

Assembling a Structure

The process of constructing and assembling a structure also affects its potential for choice and adaptability. The common practice in selling units in a housing project is to construct a model unit which is visited by interested buyers. In many projects, buyers are offered choices as to interior arrangement and the unit's finishes. The homes themselves are built only when they are sold.

When row houses are sold, construction often begins prior to the sale of the entire row. The builder can be left with unsold yet finished units. An alternative approach is to use open-web joists and to leave the interior unpartitioned and unfinished. This strategy allows greater choice at no additional cost and the fitting of the units' interiors to the clients' needs.

The chosen method of construction can also affect the degree of choice and adaptability offered. Most North American homes are built conventionally. Framers assemble precut wood segments on-site. Almost 90 percent of all building components sent to the building site are prefabricated, which in itself constitutes an initial level of flexibility in assembly.

Prefabricated construction methods have been gaining ground in woodframe, residential building construction, which will also contribute to increased choice for buyers. There are three main methods of prefabrication:

Panelized building systems facilitate and shorten the time of homebuilding in a densely built area.

modular (also known as *sectional*), *panelized,* and *precut.* Modular systems are usually entire homes, in most cases completely finished, and are shipped from the factory (where they are built in two or more sections) to the construction site where they are assembled. Since most of the work is done in a plant, only a small amount of work is left for the site. Panelized systems are factory-produced wall panels and floor sections. The wall panels are generally 8 feet high (2.5 meters) but they can range from 4 to 40 feet (1.2 to 12.2 meters). Smaller components such as windows and doors can be installed in the panels as well. There are two types of panels: *open* and *closed.* The open wall panel consists of exterior sheathing only. The other components—plumbing, electrical, insulation, and interior sheathing—are all installed on-site.

The home delivery process by prefabricators in Japan is designed for the incorporation of buyers' choices into the building process.

With the closed panel system, these components are installed at the plant, reducing construction time. In the precut system, all of the building components are prepared as a kit of parts and shipped to the site where they are assembled.

All three prefabricated methods have advantages and disadvantages with regard to adaptability during the design, construction, and use of a building. The precut system will provide greater on-site flexibility, whereas with the modular system there is little freedom to change once the home is built. All three systems, however, hold the potential for greater choice during the sale of a unit. In an integrated design and construction method commonly used in Japan, a designer meets the clients and, using a computer together with them, helps the future occupants make choices about the unit's interior layout and finishes. The choices are then sent to the factory floor, where the unit is produced and then shipped to the site (Noguchi 1999).

Prefabrication of homes offers choice and adaptability, with communication made possible through innovations in information technology methods. Prefabrication has the added advantage of considering add-on expansion. In a densely populated area where machinery access is limited, the added section can be prefabricated, shipped to the site, and hoisted and placed on a foundation wall or piers.

SERVICES

From humble beginnings at the turn of the twentieth century, when only a few homes were linked to a communal water supply and sewer systems, today's home is connected to many services. These include, among other amenities, fresh water supply, drains, electricity, natural gas (where applicable), telephone, and cable television. As technology has advanced in recent decades, the need has grown to change and manipulate these utilities as they affect the adaptability of a dwelling or an entire building. This section deals with large-scale aspects related to these systems and their effect on the dwelling unit itself.

In general, all homes are connected in various ways to different services. The line—whether it is a water main or a natural gas pipe—runs in front of the house, while others run in the rear. The location of the services themselves can be underground or above ground. Connections of drains and water mains are likely to be under the front lawn, the sidewalk, and the street. The main entry for some services is on the lower level (ground floor or basement). For other services, like cable TV or electricity, a connection is made to the building itself. From their entry location, these services are distributed to various locations in the building.

As for the home itself, at the turn of the century pipes and wires were frequently installed outside the walls or floors. In the construction boom that followed the Second World War, when building codes began to emerge, builders were required to place them inside the walls. The need to have continuous service access to pipes and to replace them when they become obsolete has become a key criterion in determining the building's adaptability.

Locating a Mechanical Room

The mechanical room in a single-family dwelling is commonly located in the basement, when one exists, or on the ground floor. In this room, one finds the heating system, hot water tank, and frequently, the main electrical panel. The location of these systems on the lower level frees the upper floor for changes when needed. When a single-family dwelling is divided into several units, placing the mechanical room where it can easily be accessible will facilitate such a process. One such location could be next to an exterior wall with an entry door from the outside. During the functioning of the unit as a single-family dwelling the door would also provide for direct access by service personnel without the need to enter the house itself.

Fishing Conduits

The tendency in the design of multistory dwellings is to stack the wet functions. For ease of construction and for economic reasons, all of the bathrooms and kitchens are placed in the same location on each floor. Such a repetitive arrangement greatly limits choice and adaptability which results in identical unit layouts. Design methods and technologies that provide the freedom to locate wet functions wherever one wants are available. Two products can be integrated to assist in this endeavor: open-web joists (previously described) and flexible PVC pipes.

Cross-linked polyethylene tubing is an alternative to copper or cast-iron pipes in hot and cold water distribution systems. The pipe is made of a 3D molecule that is more resistant to temperature extremes, chemical attack, and creep deformation. It requires fewer fittings to install, due to the fact that changes in direction can easily be accomplished without any special tools by simply curving the flexible pipe around any obstacles that are encountered. The need for elbows is thereby eliminated—a feature not found in traditional rigid pipe materials such as PVC and copper.

With regard to expansion, cross-linked pipe is able to stretch slightly in order to accommodate for the expansion of freezing water. When the ice thaws, the pipe returns to its original size, making it freeze- and crack-resistant. The sizes that are available are $\frac{3}{8}$, $\frac{1}{2}$, $\frac{5}{8}$, $\frac{3}{4}$, and 1 inch (9.4, 12.5, 15.6, 18.8, and 25 mm). The tubing is copper size, meaning that the actual outside diameter of the tube is the same nominal size as copper pipes.

The pipe is installed with a crimp ring system that is simple to assemble and requires no glues, solder, torches, or lubricants. Metallic inserts and black copper crimp rings are used as fittings which are made with a full-circle crimp tool by compressing a copper crimp ring around the tubing. This compression creates a connection by pressing the tubing into the spaces between the ribs of the fitting insert.

Flexible tubing in a residential plumbing application.

Polyvinylchloride (PVC) plumbing pipes have gained widespread use in home building and have replaced cast iron and copper plumbing, which were hard to handle and required soldering. They are used for hot and cold water and allow quick fitting, upgrading, and servicing. They also simplify the location of the wet functions anywhere on the floor and the ability to feed conduits to them easily. When needed, changes can be made to these functions by the first and subsequent occupants.

Creating a Vertical Shaft

In a multistory, multifamily structure where flexible choice of unit arrangement is offered, the design strategy needs to allow for the easy distribution of utilities. One such strategy is to create a vertical shaft that runs the height of the building. The location and dimensions of the shaft must not obstruct future changes.

A vertical shaft that feeds main utilities to each floor in a multistory arrangement can be adjacent to the stairs.

In a semidetached or row house configuration, the location can be next to the common wall where it will be accessible in the event of a systems upgrade. The distribution into the unit itself can be at the meeting point between the shaft and the floor. The conduits can pass through the open-web part of the joists into their assigned location on the floor. When dwelling units are combined or divided prior to or following occupancy, easy access to the main systems must be arranged to simplify change.

INTERIOR SPACE AND UTILITIES 5

Once the construction of the structural envelope ends, partitioning the home and completing the interior begin. The envelope and the interior are interrelated, yet, for the sake of clarity in this book, the interior is being dealt with separately. This chapter walks the reader through large and small decisions and strategies that, when taken at the conception stage, will facilitate adaptability of the home's interior. At the outset, large-scale issues are examined. These include spatial zones, layout strategies, circulation, the design of the rooms themselves, as well as design for growth and division of indoor spaces. The chapter ends by examining the home's subcomponents.

Manipulation of spaces

Functional zones	Refers to how the overall space of a dwelling unit can be arranged according to zones (e.g., public, private, daytime, nighttime) to allow a greater degree of adaptability
Spatial configurations and strategies	Relates to specific design strategies and configurations that permit a space to be easily adaptable at a macrolevel
Access to and circulation between or within spaces	Considers how circulation between and through spaces and entry into them will affect adaptability

Spatial arrangement

Function of rooms and auxiliary spaces	Analysis of how each room and its unique use, as well as auxiliary spaces, can be arranged to become more adaptable

Growth (add-in) and division

Growth	Explores the possibility of home design, where unused indoor spaces will later be added into the main space
Division	Considers design strategies whereby a space will be divided to make room for a new use or an independent-dwelling unit

Manipulation of subcomponents

Technology of and access to utilities	Describes the means by which the home's interior utilities, their placement, and access to them, once installed, will affect adaptability
Interior premanufactured components	Introduces and explores premanufactured components, such as demountable partitions, for their installation and use in achieving adaptability in the home's interior
Surface finishes	Considers the effect that occupants have in choosing surface finishes, such as for the walls or floors, and their effect on adaptability

Subjects that have been considered in the study of issues that affect the interior adaptability of a home.

FUNCTIONAL ZONES

A basic step in the interior design of a home is to establish *zones.* The zones correspond with the functions of the unit and can be divided into public, semipublic, or private areas. A designer often places the private functions (for example, bedrooms) at a more discrete place at the back of the house, away from the entry door and high-traffic areas. Zones can also be distinguished by daytime and nighttime activities, according to the periods of their main uses. Decisions as to where to place each zone will depend, among other factors, on the orientation of the home. It is common, for example, to place a bedroom along the northern, less sunny side of the house, since the space will be used during the night. The public functions—kitchen or living room—will be placed against the southern facade for daylight exposure and passive solar gain.

Decisions about the placement of zones influence adaptability and are made when the overall layout of the dwelling is conceived. They determine how difficult it might be to switch things around later in the home's life cycle.

Balancing Areas

When, in the course of the design, the location and area of zones are decided upon, balancing their sizes can be a future advantage. It could happen that a need may arise to turn a front daytime zone containing a living room and dining space, for example, into a bedroom area as part of a comprehensive rearrangement of the home's layout. Having zones of equal size can be an advantage as it will limit the need for a major overhaul and even prevent demolition.

Placing Wet Functions

The location of wet functions will influence the exchange of areas between zones. When the kitchen or the bathroom is an integral part of one of the zones, it will be hard to change the zone's use and character. Moving wet functions is a cumbersome and costly task, which is not attempted very often. It is therefore better to place these functions in a neutral area between the

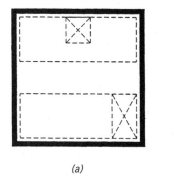 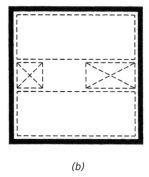

(a)   (b)

Locating wet functions between zones facilitates adaptability by
eliminating the need to relocate them when changes in the zones
themselves occur. (*a*) Within zones, (*b*) between zones.

zones. If, in the future, the occupants decide to expand their home and to
adapt old uses, the locations of the bathroom and kitchen will not be an
obstacle to the process.

Zones in a Two-Story Home

The two-story home permits the division of functions into two distinct zones,
each located on its own level. Public uses are often located on the lower,
entrance floor, and the private areas on the upper. When a basement exists, it
can accommodate utility functions such as a mechanical room or laundry. Lin-
ing up plumbing pipes and bathrooms, as well as allocating space and installing
conduits for a future kitchen on the upper floor will facilitate the transformation
of a single-family dwelling to a two-family structure.

The Right Exposure

The tendency in the design of a space is to relate the openings in the facade, as
well as their number and size, to its purpose. This approach limits the use of the
zone or the room to a single function. Providing greater exposure in the form of
larger or a greater number of windows is always preferable when the need for
adaptability is sought. It is a double-edged sword, since more windows will raise

construction costs and decrease the energy efficiency of the unit. Therefore, a careful assessment of the openings must be made in order to reach a balance between exposure to natural light and future adaptability.

SPATIAL CONFIGURATIONS AND STRATEGIES

When the design of a home begins, one of the initial steps is to determine its overall dimensions and those of the perimeter walls. This decision will be influenced, among others, by the designer's concept as well as by zoning bylaws. Once the proportions have been determined, the main zones within the dwelling will be set. The next stage is to explore concepts and strategies for the zones themselves: to determine how these spaces will be designed to be adaptable at the pre- or postoccupancy stages. The designer must choose among several strategies that will permit such a process to occur. The chosen strategy can be applied to the entire dwelling, a single zone, or even one room within it.

Wide Open Space

A strategy that ensures that room for change will be available is to leave open space: to try to avoid partitions that enclose and define functions and activities. There are functions around which walls are required, such as a bathroom. Yet the partitioning of other spaces in the house is often the result of household composition or cultural habits.

In the early part of the twentieth century, traditional home design created, defined, and enclosed space for each use. Accordingly, the kitchen was separated by walls from the dining room and parlor. Over the years, new design trends emerged. Cooking ceased to be an isolated activity, and the kitchen often became part of the dining or family area. The living room was also integrated in this arrangement to make a large open space for the public or semipublic functions. The rise of the nontraditional household has made open-space design more common. It can be argued that a single person might need a minimal number of walls in the private zone since acoustic separation and privacy are less of a concern.

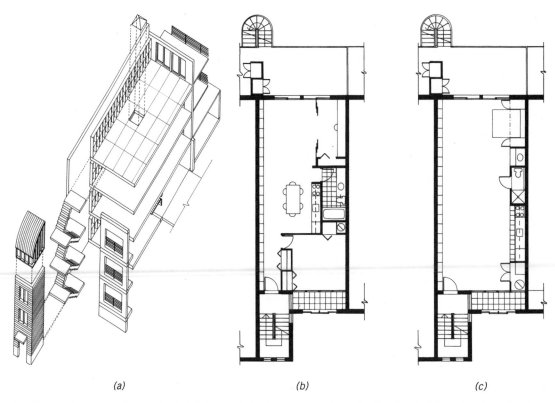

In this multistory row house design (a), the stairs have been placed in the front of the structure, freeing the floor for an open concept. Several options [Alternative A (*b*) and Alternative B (*c*)] with varying degrees of openness have been offered.

Which space to leave open is often a matter of trends and also depends on the dwelling type. There are house types that lend themselves easily to the open-space concept. The rancher, for example, is such a prototype. Since all of the functions are located on the same level, combining the public functions is relatively simple and will facilitate future changes. The two-story home also provides an opportunity for open-space design in the lower level where public uses can be located and combined. At a later stage, if that level is to be turned into an independent unit, partitioning the space will not require extensive demolition and changes. To facilitate future alterations in an open concept, attention needs to be paid to several aspects. In a multistory house, stairs should be placed along the longitudinal wall rather than in the middle of the room. It is also recommended not to change the elevations of the floor levels themselves.

Arrangements whereby all the functions are located on the same floor without a change in floor level will permit an easy interchange between them.

Multipurpose Spaces

Creating multipurpose spaces is another design strategy that lets future adaptability take place. The objective of this approach is to design rooms with dimensions and proportions that allow a variety of functions to occur within them. The very same room could serve as a bedroom, a living room, or as a home office at different life stages by the original or subsequent occupants.

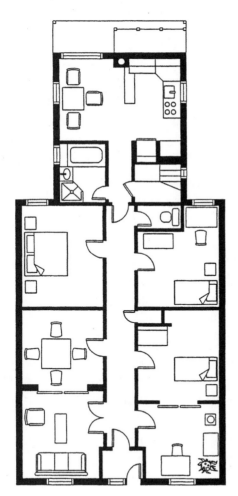

In the late nineteenth century, designers of traditional plexes created rooms of equal-dimension sizes that let occupants decide their uses and the changes to them later during the occupancy. Due to their adaptable character, these units undergo very little transformation over the years.

The practice of designing residences with multipurpose spaces was common in traditional designs. Montreal architects used this approach at the beginning of the twentieth century while designing plexes. The multifamily building was often purchased by a single owner who resided on the ground floor and rented the upper dwellings. Each unit had its own direct staircase and entrance, eliminating the need for a common walk-up stair shaft. In the layout, the service functions of the unit (i.e., kitchen, laundry, and bathroom) were placed in the rear, while the front end contained the other functions in a multipurpose-room setup. This design approach suited the use of the dwelling for rental purposes, as occupants chose to arrange the room functions according to their unique household composition and needs. The vitality of this dwelling type and design approach still holds true today, as the interior of the units needed very few modifications to suit contemporary lifestyles.

There are several guidelines that a designer needs to bear in mind when conceiving multipurpose spaces and rooms. The room's dimensions and proportions are perhaps the most important aspects. In general, the larger the space is, the wider the options for adaptability will be. Since ample space is not always available, one must therefore envision the types of uses that the same room could accommodate: functions like the living room, master bedroom, or dining room. A dimension of 15 by 15 feet (4.6 by 4.6 meters) will likely facilitate all of these functions. In small homes, the area could be reduced to 12 by 12 feet (3.7 by 3.7 meters). When proportions are decided, a square would be desirable since it presents fewer limitations on furniture arrangements.

The permanent interior features of a room will also affect its multipurpose use. A room with a closet will be recognized as a bedroom, for example. Eliminating these identifying features will facilitate a variety of uses. As for storage or closet space, in European housing the occupants bring their own cupboards with them when they move in and take them away when they leave.

Having ample light to accommodate a range of uses is another aspect that must be considered in the process of designing multipurpose space. A living room, where households spend their daytime, will require a greater amount of natural light than a bedroom, where most activities take place after the sun has set. Decisions about the number of windows and their dimensions therefore need to take into consideration the range of uses of the room.

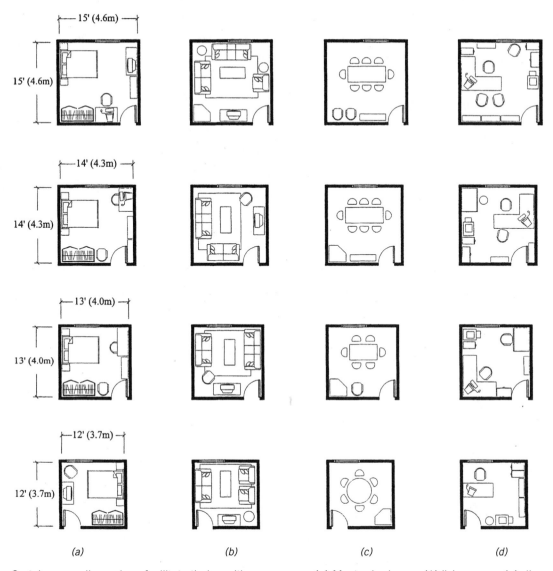

Certain room dimensions facilitate their multipurpose use. (a) Master bedroom, (b) living room, (c) dining room, (d) home office.

When these principles are followed, the home can become a true life-cycle home, when the use of its rooms is changed along with the needs of the occupants.

Furniture as Walls

Design for the use of furniture to subdivide spaces and to create distinct functions within a large room is another strategy for adaptability. This approach is based on the notion that contemporary building technology offers possibilities to distinguish between the home's enclosure and interior by eliminating the need for bearing partitions. The space can therefore remain open and adaptable to the needs of its occupants.

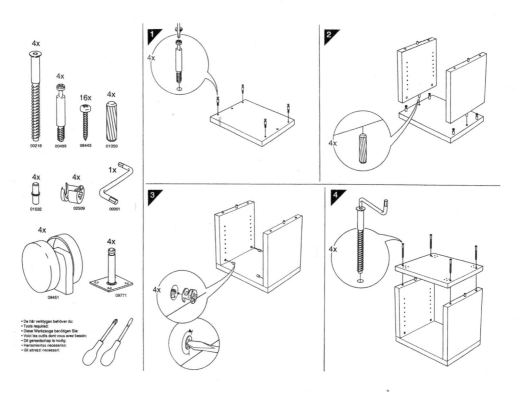

A simplified manufacturing process and clear instructions have popularized self-assembly furniture.

The introduction of new building technologies was accompanied by lifestyle trends and demographic changes that gave rise to smaller households for whom conventional interior subdivision using permanent walls could be reconsidered. Expenses associated with building walls and then spending additional sums of money on furnishing these spaces could be reduced to a single task of using the furniture itself as dividers.

A parallel evolution is taking place in the development of the furniture itself. In the past half-century, the industry has moved from custom-made to mass production. The use of plastic and composite boards has contributed to lowering the cost of furniture and the creation of a variety of choices for homeowners suitable to their needs and budgets. Furniture and renovation centers now offer packaged bookshelves and closet components for self-assembly, all of which can become space dividers.

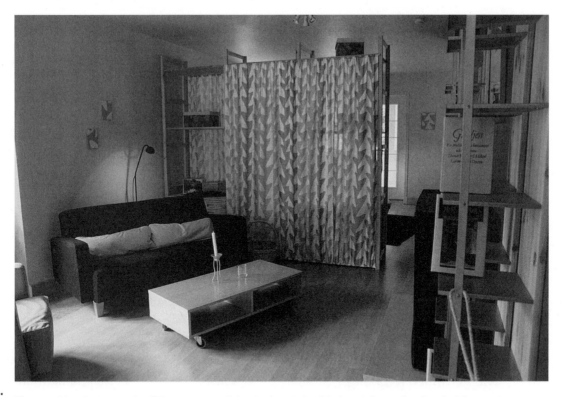

The partition between the living room and the bedroom in this home is made of a shelving system.

Several aspects must be considered when designing a space for subdivision with furniture. Where to locate the furniture and which function it can enclose will be prime issues. Wet functions are likely to be enclosed with conventional partitions. Other functions (e.g., a study, a bedroom, and a dining area) can all be made of furnishings.

Another consideration is the placement of electrical switches and sockets. Codes require their installation on permanent walls, and with the absence of interior partitions, primarily on the dwelling's exterior enclosure. Similar to commercial buildings, an alternative location would be to have sockets installed in the floor, when the code permits such a practice. Another possibility for some of the spaces is to have suspended-ceiling track lighting to which electrical appliances or light fixtures can be plugged.

When a single person is the occupant of a space where furniture is used as partitions, noise may not constitute a concern. When more than one occupant shares the space, reducing sound transmission is a challenge. Limiting the hard surfaces is a common approach to reducing noise in any space, especially in the home without walls. Using wall-to-wall carpets or area rugs is a common solution. Another approach would be to affix acoustic boards or padding to the back of vertical dividers, which could be clothing cupboards or bookshelves.

Similarly, privacy will be of lesser importance in a single-person household. Yet it could be an important consideration when a small family or unrelated occupants share the dwelling. Space-dividing furniture can therefore be as low as 3 feet (0.9 meter) or as tall as 7 feet (2.1 meters), as needed. Doors and doorframes can be purchased and placed between space dividers when necessary.

ACCESS TO AND CIRCULATION BETWEEN OR WITHIN SPACES

A substantial portion of a home's space is devoted to circulation. These areas link one function to another and can be regarded as lost usable areas. Common design approaches attempt to reduce the circulation area or to make them part of other functions in the home. The passage to the kitchen, for example, can be made through the living room. When a homeowner undertakes alterations, circulation will very often determine the extent of changes. A well-thought-out movement network will reduce the need for extensive work and will make small changes to the home's layout or to the rooms within it a simple matter.

Crossing a Zone

When circulation arteries pass through zones, changing the home's layout will require extensive alterations. The need to walk through the living or family room to the bedroom area, for example, will hamper the uses of these spaces. Several strategies can be used in the design of passages that will not limit change. Mov-

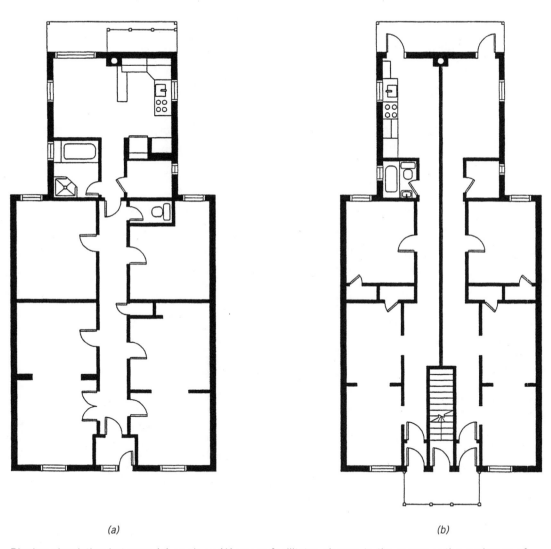

(a) *(b)*

Placing circulation between (*a*) or along (*b*) zones facilitates change to the rooms or the exchange of functions between them.

ing between zones rather than through them is one approach. A double-loaded corridor is created with functions on both sides. Changes can take place within or between the zones without the corridor becoming an obstacle. In a semidetached or row house arrangement, the corridor can be placed along the longitudinal wall. Once again, passage to and from the rooms will not take place through them.

Where to Locate Stairs

In a multilevel house, once the location of the stairs has been decided, their placement will influence the layout in general and movements in particular on all levels throughout the home's life cycle. Locating stairs in the right spot is therefore a critical decision as far as future adaptability is concerned.

If a prime objective is to shorten the length of corridors, the stairs can be located close to the entrance. The rest of the space can be freed up for manipulation. Placing the stairs against the front facade, however, will limit the view and natural exposure from this elevation. The designer therefore needs to reach a compromise between future adaptability and functionality.

Using the stairs as a wedge between rooms will limit restrictions to changes within these spaces. Another strategy is to place them close to the entrance in the middle between two zones. A front foyer will allow access space into the

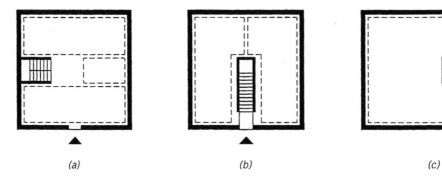

(a)   (b)   (c)

Locations of stairs that minimize interruptions to spaces and increase their future adaptability (a) Stairs as a wedge between functions, (b) a middle location of a long straight run, (c) stairs as an appendix to the main space.

rooms as well as clothes storage. When the home has a basement, the same stair shaft will lead to that level. Yet another strategy is to create a stair shaft either within or outside the structure. This alternative not only frees up the interior space, but simplifies the process of dividing a multilevel structure into independent units on each floor.

In a semidetached house or in a row house, when the unit has a long and narrow configuration, a preferred location for the stairs is along the common wall. This placement frees the main spaces and prevents the obstruction of light penetration from both front and rear facades.

Hallways and Corridors as Adaptable Spaces

An accepted notion by designers and homeowners is that the only function of hallways and corridors is to link rooms. Given the fact that circulation space can account for up to 30 percent of a home's floor space, a single use could be considered as not taking full advantage of a valuable area. It could also limit adaptability. When designed properly, corridors can serve more than one purpose.

At various stages of the family life cycle, there is commonly a need for additional storage space. Hallways and corridors can serve such a purpose. When 48 inches (1.2 meters) are allocated to corridor width, 12 inches (0.3 meters) of them can be used for storage, leaving sufficient area for passage. Shallow cupboards and shelves can be used for linens, books, and other small household belongings. When the family gets smaller, these storage spaces can be demounted if they are not needed.

When a small house is designed for vertical expansion, the corridor can initially accommodate storage cupboards. Later, these cupboards could be replaced by stairs leading to a new upper level.

The spacing of entry doors to rooms along the corridor should also be considered. The designer needs to ensure that adequate continuous wall area will be available to make such storage functional.

The width of the corridor in this home permits the installation of storage cupboards and shelves.

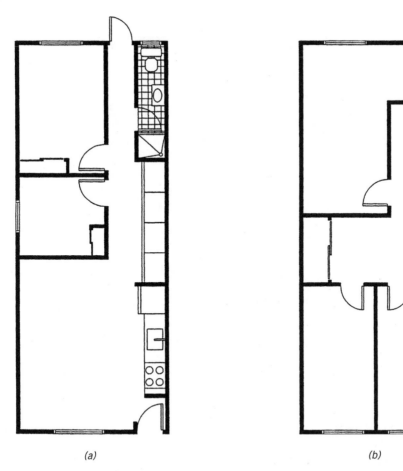

(a)   (b)

A storage space along the corridor (a) of this low-cost home was designed to be replaced by stairs leading to a future expanded upper level (b).

Circulation Between Levels

When a multifamily, multistory building is designed with the consideration of combining units on different levels into a single dwelling, the designer must pay attention to circulation between the levels. The placement of stairs to the upper level should allow for the simple introduction of a passageway between floors. The very same strategy should permit a situation where a large unit is to be divided. Passage to the new space or to the upper level should not take place through the space of a frequently used function.

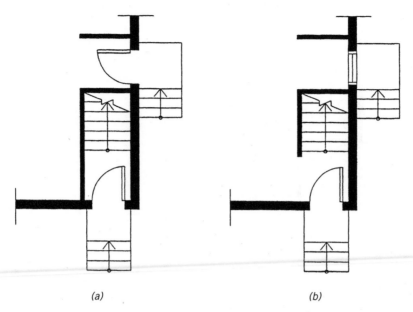

(a)   *(b)*

The thoughtful placement of the entry doors in a two-family house (*a*) simplifies the introduction of a passageway and its conversion into a single-family dwelling (*b*).

Locating an Entry Door to a Room

Several principles need to be borne in mind when an entry door to a room is placed. The process begins by assessing the location of the entry doors to other rooms in the same zone. The desire is often to shorten corridor length and assemble all the entrances in the same area, leaving more space for the rooms themselves. A paramount criterion will be the influence of the entry on the use itself. When considering adaptability, the designer would be better off to disregard a particular function and to think about several uses for the same room. Rules governing the placement of doors therefore need to be general in nature.

Locating the door close to a side wall rather than in the middle has several advantages. First, it permits the introduction of another door later and the division of a large room into two spaces. Second, it leaves the space uninterrupted by circulation. It also leaves large expanses of wall area against which furniture

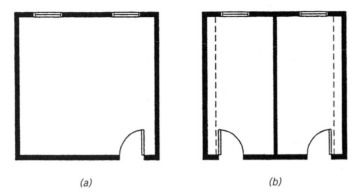

(a)   (b)

Placing a door close to a corner (*a*) will simplify the introduction of another door and the division of the room into two (*b*).

can be placed, thereby allowing a variety of uses to take place. When the door is placed along the side wall, leaving a minimum of 15 inches (375 millimeters) behind it will facilitate the future installation of shallow storage furniture, such as a bookshelf, behind the door.

FUNCTION OF ROOMS AND AUXILIARY SPACES

Once the placement of the zones has been decided upon, and a strategy to arrange and reach the rooms within them has been selected, the process begins of locating the rooms themselves according to their unique function and interior layout. The mind-set that guides the design of such rooms can regard them and their uses as permanent, whereby the activities within them are less likely to change. Alternatively, a designer could view their layout at the time of design as the first snapshot in a life cycle that continues to evolve. This section follows the latter approach. The concepts and design proposals outlined here are meant to provide the occupant with choices prior to moving in, and room for change in their homes as often as they need it. In a mobile society, subsequent occupants may wish to rearrange the rooms according to their own needs. Therefore, a strategy for long-term intervention is demonstrated. In the latter part of this section, several frequently used spaces and activities have been selected to illustrate these principles.

Room for Evolution

Reflection on the need to change and adapt the interior of homes makes one recognize that life imposes a certain frequency on the process. The need for transformations can occur *daily*. Often, these are small changes (e.g., moving a chest of drawers from one end of the room to the other or reorganizing the contents of a storage space). There are also *seasonal* changes. The placement of the furniture in a room to suit a desired sun exposure in winter or summer is an example of one such change. Then there are the *yearly* changes, those that happen as a result of significant changes to family composition or a change of household financial circumstances that trigger a need or opportunity to undertake more extensive alterations. Some of these changes can be predicted and others may occur at random.

There are also external pressures to change. Along with transformations in society's demographic makeup, lifestyles, and cultural attitudes, rooms in homes—and their layouts and uses—have also evolved. Led by innovations in information and appliance technology, and fueled by consumerism, today's homes look different from those built a few decades ago. Not only have the rooms themselves changed, but the relationship between them has altered. Rooms in some homes assume more than one use. Kitchens can be the place for kids' homework and bedrooms a place to watch TV late at night. A living room in some homes may contain a wall of books and in others an array of electronic gadgets. A study for some may be a desk in the hallway or, for others, a home office connected to electronic mail. The many options possible can be read as a menu from which a home buyer can choose. Selections need not end at the time of purchase but can continue throughout the occupancy.

This mind-set is accompanied by an evolution in the construction of home interiors. Custom-designed cabinetry or flooring is still present in many homes, but most, primarily homes in tract developments, use premanufactured products. Choosing and fitting has become simpler as the industry has changed. What must be thought of and designed for is the backstage: the rooms' locations, dimensions, proportions, and utilities to accommodate these products.

The Work of a Room

When one analyzes the work of a room, a distinction can be made between the *principal* and *auxiliary* activities. The principal activity represents the main functions of a place: cooking in the kitchen, sleeping in bedrooms, and washing clothes in the laundry room are some examples. Auxiliary activities can also take place in these rooms: preparing homework or paying bills in the kitchen, watching TV in the bedroom, and ironing in the laundry room.

Each of these principal activities has its own furnishings through which the main activity is carried out. A bed in the bedroom and cabinets and countertops in the kitchen are trivial examples. However, there can be other space allocations and hardware to support the auxiliary activities. Watching TV in the bedroom requires a television stand. Storing clothes and linens requires closet space and a chest of drawers.

During design, deciding on what the principal activity of a space will be is a relatively simple task. The auxiliary activities and the furnishings that support them are often difficult to know. They likely depend on the household composition, lifestyle, and habits. A recommended strategy, therefore, is to design space to accommodate the principal activity and to allow, when possible, the occupants to choose the hardware for the auxiliary activities. It is also likely that the principal activity of a space will be long lasting, while the auxiliary activities will change along with the needs of the homeowner.

Kitchen

New technologies and lifestyle trends have contributed to the continuous evolution of kitchen design. The kitchen has become a highly versatile space in a modern household and one of the main rooms that buyers scrutinize when they are about to purchase a new home. The range of activities that take place in the kitchen also make it a high-priority space for choice and adaptability.

Several functions in kitchens have changed in the last few decades and are likely to continue to evolve. At the heart of the evolution is the time pressure that is put on the family when both heads of the household work outside the home. Time allocated for food preparation has shrunk. The share of ready-to-serve food has increased on the dining tables of many households. These phenomena have several consequences. There has been a continuous increase in the space allocated to storage. Whether it is cold or dry storage, more pantry and freezer space has had to be created. The volume of refrigerators has expanded as the freezer part of them has grown.

Another sphere of activity that has undergone change is the cooking itself. The microwave has taken a central role in the kitchen, surpassing the stovetop. It has gradually moved from its own side cabinet to the countertop to be installed among the cupboards themselves. The microwave is one of the several appliances and gadgets, introduced periodically by appliance manufacturers, that have caused kitchen space and the countertop to swell in size.

A range of activities—old and new—has contributed to the reconfiguration of kitchen design. The space has maintained its centrality in the house, yet new chores have been added, the result of a hectic lifestyle. In small homes, the washer and dryer are often located in the kitchen, which requires its own plumbing arrangement. The dining activity has also become part of the kitchen, leaving the formal dining area for use on festive occasions only. The kitchen's dining table, in homes with small children, has become a place where homework is prepared after dinner and where bills are paid and other household chores take place after hours. Communication technology has gradually found its way into kitchens, with cordless telephones, small television sets, and even places for laptop computers and fax machines.

Over the years, kitchen cabinetry has evolved from custom-made to modular production. First, a finished shell that includes electricity, plumbing, and flooring is prepared. Then cabinets, ordered from a catalog, are sent preassembled to the site, where they are mounted on the walls, leaving space for appliances to be brought and plugged in. This mode of construction simplifies the process of change, when necessary.

When the design of an adaptable kitchen is undertaken, several aspects need to be considered. On a macroscale, the designer must bear in mind the distinction between principal and auxiliary activities, which was outlined previously. Food preparation and its variety of tasks and devices will be the principal chore. Other activities will depend on the household itself. To accommodate a choice of kitchen layouts, as the principal activity, the placement of the main electrical appliances (oven, refrigerator, microwave, dishwasher), as well as the sink and its pipes, must be carefully approached. Flexible polyvinyl chloride (PVC) plumbing now facilitates the extension of lines from the main hot- and cold-water pipes to any loca-

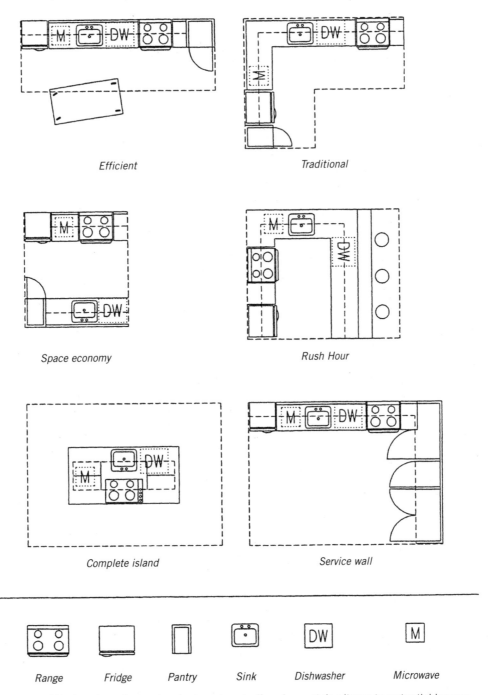

Efficient

Traditional

Space economy

Rush Hour

Complete island

Service wall

| Range | Fridge | Pantry | Sink | DW Dishwasher | M Microwave |

A variety of kitchen layouts can be designed and offered as catalog items to potential buyers in particular projects.

tion on the floor. The introduction of electrical raceways running above the countertop along the kitchen wall also allows the hookup of appliances anywhere.

Extensive changes in kitchens often involve the replacement of all the cabinets. This is also an opportunity to change the kitchen layout. To provide more design options, ample natural light in the form of large openings needs to be designed. A balance must be struck between windows and wall areas, since more windows will decrease mounting space for cabinets. Another issue to be addressed is circulation. The location of the exit door in a neutral spot will free the peripheral area for work.

Once these basic principles have been followed, a range of kitchen layouts to fill a variety of household compositions and budgets can be offered. The working surface, for example, can be expanded by using a rolling counter, while in another layout a complete island for small households is suggested. A service wall–style of kitchen is also available to provide storage space for hardware such as a TV, washer and dryer, even a small desk and stool.

Living, Family, Media

Another part of the home that has undergone a transformation as a result of technological and lifestyle trends is the living area. The living space encompasses several rooms or functions. It includes the living room itself and its own seating arrangements and auxiliary activities. In some homes, there might also be a media room, a space delegated to house all of the electronic equipment. The principal activity there is family interaction, listening to music, watching TV, or using a computer. Then there is the family room, which, for some, extends and replicates the living room in a less formal arrangement. In a home with toddlers, it could be the play area along with toys or a playpen under the watchful eye of a parent working in the kitchen. Some homes may contain all of these rooms, while others have only a single room with a mixture of functions within it.

Activities that involve interaction with telecommunication hardware have increased their share significantly in home life. Elements related to entertainment and the media can potentially offer something to everyone in the household, any time and in any room. These facilities are fast becoming common auxiliary activities in many rooms of the home. Watching TV, for example, takes place in kitchens, bedrooms, and in living and family areas. The same communication devices (TV, DVD, stereo, computer), which can serve to separate household members, can just as easily function as integrative sources, as anchors of spaces that are capable of bringing the household together. When the location of the main or only TV, computer, or stereo in the home is the living or family room of the house, appropriate care is therefore to be taken in the design of this space in order to accommodate the particular needs and priorities of each household.

Past trends suggest that innovation will continue to fuel the production of electronic devices. With new gadgets making their appearance on a regular basis, the need to design the living area for constant change is evident. Since in most homes the living and the family rooms are already open spaces, attention must be paid to upgrading subcomponents such as wiring. New homes are now wired with computer and cable TV jacks in every room. These systems need to be installed with easy access to allow for the insertion of new wiring and the removal of old wiring.

Bathroom

Along with the kitchen, the bathroom is closely inspected when decisions about the purchase of a home are made. From humble beginnings at the turn of the twentieth century, with exposed plumbing, this space has been reinvented to contain a larger area and an array of costly and highly efficient fixtures. Most new homes and apartments in North America have more than one bathroom, with a main one and others that act as auxiliaries to rooms such as the master bedroom, the family room, and a powder room adjacent to the entrance. In a multistory space, a bathroom is likely to be found on each level.

Efficiency of use and a trend to turn the bathroom into a house spa were the key reasons for the reconfiguration of the space. The use of the room by several members of the household during morning "rush hours" has contributed to the introduction of a second sink. Quiet, water-conserving toilets have replaced old models, and whirlpool bathtubs are also common. Innovations keep being introduced, with predictions of the bathroom taking on a therapeutic role as the number of elderly in society increases.

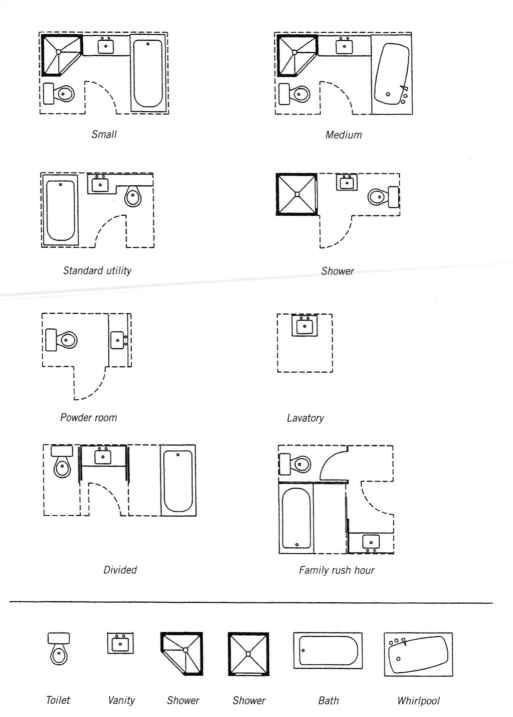

Small

Medium

Standard utility

Shower

Powder room

Lavatory

Divided

Family rush hour

Toilet   Vanity   Shower   Shower   Bath   Whirlpool

Bathroom layouts need to be designed to offer choices that reflect the household structure as well as particular locations in the home.

The bathroom is one of the rooms in the house that also undergoes periodic extensive renovations. The introduction of new fixtures and the will of the first and subsequent homeowners to personalize the space have made builders offer choices to buyers prior to occupancy. Here, too, the room has to be prepared for adaptability, primarily at the subcomponent level. The introduction of flexible PVC piping (discussed earlier in the section entitled "Kitchen") has facilitated the relocation of fixtures. An access panel for the bathtub is also essential. The possibility of accessing and servicing drainage also needs to be accounted for. Installing horizontal service panels under a bathtub or shower stall, accessible from the floor below, can be a way to access these plumbing conduits.

As for the cabinetry, today's cupboards are built and sold as integrated units with a mirror and sink. The designer must make sure that the wall area behind them will contain plumbing pipes that might need to be accessed in the future.

Home Office

Transformations in the forms of employment and the development of electronic means of communication have combined to introduce the home office. Full-time work from home has become common for many. Home offices are also used for part-time activities that complement a person's regular day job, or for simple household chores such as paying a bill or sending an e-mail.

When a home office for full-time employment is needed, another room in the house may be converted, and several aspects will have to be considered. The room must provide basic space for tasks such as storing documents, a place for a computer desk, and space for a visiting client, if need be. The room must be located away but not fully secluded from the rest of the house. It has to offer a view onto the street to enhance social interactions. The home office could be in a secondary space in the house, such as the attic or any elevated basement with its own entrance. It must have ample natural light and good connections to utilities. The placement of these utilities can be made in advance in the entire house, or the installation of appropriate access cable raceways can allow their introduction later on.

With the continuous proliferation of electronic communication and lifestyle advantages that at-home work provides, home offices are here to stay. Design-

Minimal

Minimal plus

Extended minimal

Graphic station

Compact office

Large office

Filing   Shelves   Computer   Printer   Fax   Copier

A home office or study can be a self-contained room with direct access to the outside, or it can be a nook in the corner of another room, functioning as an auxiliary activity in the room.

ers and builders should therefore consider and offer them along with other choices to home buyers.

Storage

The demand for storage space in homes has grown significantly in recent decades. A result of rampant consumerism and the introduction of new affordable goods, the need for storage space in every room has grown. Here, too, the quantity and type of needed storage depends on the household. A large family will tend to store more than a single-person household; therefore, the quantity of storage as well as its makeup may vary. The choices range from leaving a room bare and allowing the occupants to purchase and bring along their own cupboards, to fully equipped setups that contain an assortment of prefabricated adjustable components.

Regardless of the choice, with the exception of a storage room, storage is an auxiliary activity. It could be the storing of clothing in a bedroom or hygienic products in the bathroom. Evolution has taken place in storage spaces in homes.

From a simple shelf and rod for hanging clothes in the bedroom, storage areas now have their own walk-in closets. Within these spaces, fittings are now available to adjust the arrangement of the storage to the special needs of the occupants. More shelves, for example, will be available in one room, as opposed to more drawers in another. Other types of storage may be needed in other rooms. The living room could have a wall unit for a TV as well as for books, and the laundry room could have facilities to store detergents.

Japanese home builders offer their clients a wide range of storage possibilities in the form of a shown menu when prefabricated homes are sold. These storage spaces are designed to fit budgets and family composition. As society continues to diversify on this continent, and tempting goods keep being offered, bought, and stored, attention will have to be paid to adaptable storage.

It is likely that interior design trends will continue to be introduced along with new technologies and emerging lifestyles. Designers need to bear in mind that each room has both principal and auxiliary activities. The principal use is likely to remain the same. Auxiliary activities, however, may vary, and opportunities for their transformation need to be provided.

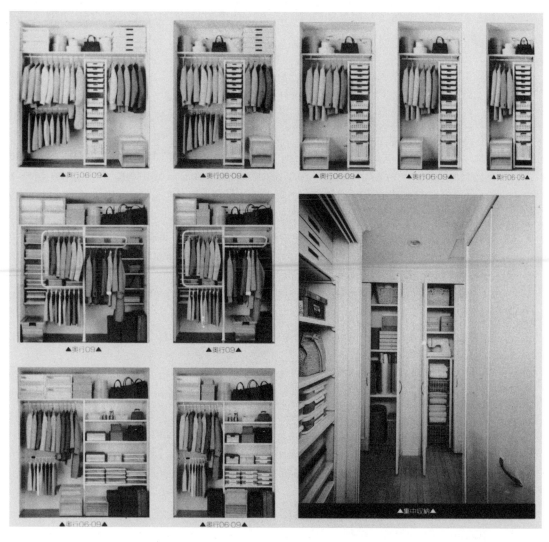

Japanese manufacturers of prefabricated homes offer their customers a wide choice of storage arrangements.

GROWTH (ADD-IN) AND DIVISION

The ability to configure a house volume in a variety of ways is another form of adaptability. A space can be expanded to annex adjacent area within the house enclosure or, alternatively, it can be divided to form separate dwelling units. Growth was dealt with earlier (i.e., the add-on concept, where exterior space is tacked onto the home or separated from it to form an independent unit). This section explores the add-in approach, where the space that is added to the unit is within the building enclosure. *Division* here refers to the conversion of one space into a few spaces, each with its own access.

Manipulating Volumes

When a home is designed and occupied, a common approach is to use the entire area within its enclosure. At times, due to a lack of means or the household's small size, the occupants might decide to use only a portion of the space and leave the rest unfinished. The remaining area will be completed and used as means become available or when the household itself grows. This process, which can happen at random or be planned for, is referred to as an *add-in* design strategy. It can take a variety of forms, the most common being expansion to the basement level or the attic.

The expansion process can be reversed. A large area on one or several levels can be divided. It can be turned from a single-dwelling unit into several, each with its own entrance. Division can also take the form of creating a new independent function within the unit, like a home office with its own access. When considering adding or dividing spaces in the design of a new home, several aspects need to be accounted for. They will be outlined and illustrated in the following three subsections.

Adding Within an Open Shell

When a home is built on a costly and small plot of land, a common-sense approach is to exploit the entire buildable area, that is, to build on all of the remaining area once setbacks have been deducted. Zoning regulations also mandate a certain building height. Thus, when a buildable volume is formed—

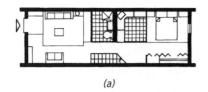

(a)

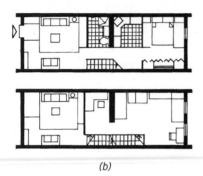

(b)

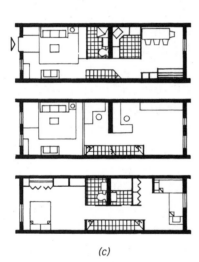

(c)

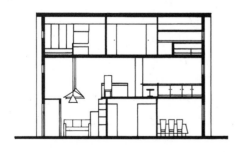

(d)

In Kiriat-Ono, Israel, architect I. M. Goodovitch designed a 46-unit development where a first floor was constructed within a shell, and an empty volume was left above for the occupants to add in later. (a) Stage A: The beginning—a young couple; (b) stage B: the couple with one or two children; (c) stage C: the couple with grown-up children; (d) cross-sectional diagram.

one that will be divided into floors and occupied by one or several families—the use of the created volume can take different forms. One floor may be constructed within the enclosure, with the remaining floors to be built and added in later.

Such a strategy was used by architect I. M. Goodovitch in his row housing project in Kiriat-Ono, Israel. This 46-unit development offered vertical expansion within an initial shell. The ground-related first floor was built first. Occupants, mostly young first-time buyers, added in floors later. The exterior uniformity of the project was maintained throughout the incremental growth process, although this was achieved at the expense of any opportunity for individuality. The shell, as the occupants noted, simplified the internal construction and the process of expansion. It also enabled them to spread their investment progressively over the course of the expansion at their own discretion. The narrow width—and as a result, the short span—simplified the construction of the additions.

Introducing a Mezzanine

Taking advantage of a high ceiling is another add-in strategy. The practice is common in the conversion of industrial building spaces into dwellings (known as lofts), and can also be applied to new homes. The designer introduces a *mezzanine*—a space that will be left unfinished initially—or will make arrangements for the introduction of one later in the occupancy. A mezzanine in many North American jurisdictions is permitted to occupy up to 40 percent of the area below. Therefore, the space is often only sufficient to accommodate a bedroom or home office. The mezzanine is also open to the area below, thereby creating a continuous space from lower to upper levels.

When designing for the future introduction of a mezzanine, height will be an important consideration. A minimum clearance of 16 feet (4.9 meters) is desired for the purpose. The structure may be designed with a pitched roof, and in some of the mezzanine's area the height may vary. Another consideration is circulation. Some municipalities require that conventional stairs reach the mezzanine, and according to other codes, a stepladder may be used. For either of these alternatives, a place for their installation needs to be prepared in advance.

The San Francisco architect Donald MacDonald has used mezzanines in many of his designs for moderate-cost housing in the Bay area. MacDonald's

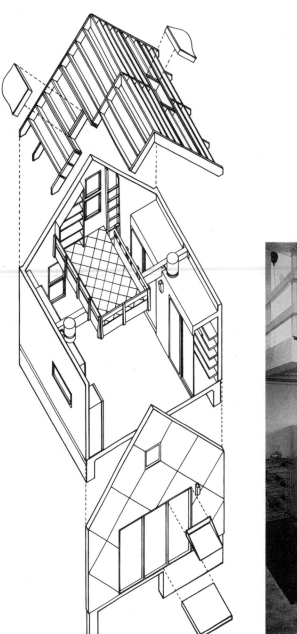

San Francisco architect Donald MacDonald includes a place for a mezzanine in much of his moderate-cost housing.

designs are characterized by an attempt to lower cost by designing small spaces that are used efficiently. The introduction of a mezzanine is a strategy that works well with his open-concept homes. The mezzanine is introduced initially or later in the occupancy, and its installation is accommodated by structural preparation in the walls and roof. The occupants, mostly nontraditional households, used the upper space for a variety of functions, with the master bedroom being the most popular.

Expanding into Unfinished Space

Growth can also take the form of a design where a portion of the dwelling will remain unfinished, into which expansion will occur later on. The unfinished space can be the second floor of a two-story dwelling, the attic, or the lower level (the basement in some homes). The degree of incompletion can range from leaving bare insulated walls without utilities to a plastered and painted enclosure without interior dividing partitions and with only extensions of utilities for future connections. According to this add-in strategy, the designer anticipates expansion and builds into the design the means to facilitate the growth. Particular design considerations will depend, of course, on the unit's typology and dimensions, yet some issues need to be considered regardless.

Openings in the space's enclosure to let in natural light will be an important consideration. In the case of a custom-designed home, future functions can be anticipated, yet it is recommended to create large numbers of generic openings, since the household's needs may change. Providing large windows for a raised basement will render the space more usable for a range of functions. In the case of an attic, the roof's angle can be designed for occupancy from the outset. To facilitate such a process, special trusses, when used, can be selected. In addition, a dormer can be designed in the front of the unit and, when the home is detached, on the attic's gable walls.

A function that is commonly anticipated on every level of a multistory house is a bathroom. In the process of installing such a function on an occupied level, a good strategy would be to extend the pipes to an unfinished upper level. This would prevent the need for demolition on a lower level in order to connect to existing plumbing lines. A similar consideration can be taken with electrical conduits. Circulation to the unoccupied level is crucial

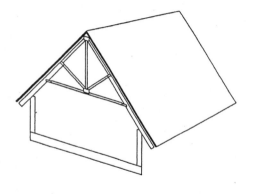
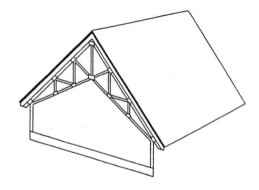

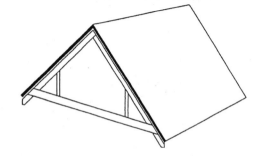

Using special, prefabricated roof trusses facilitates converting an attic into habitable space.

to the functioning of the space. Locating a downward or upward stair along a peripheral wall would free the space for partitioning, according to the desires of the occupants.

Planning for expansion to the basement or a finished but unpartitioned second floor was the strategy used in the design of the Grow Home. The narrow-front row house measured 14 feet (4.3 meters) wide and 36 feet (11 meters) long and offered interior and exterior adaptability options. These included alternatives for basement arrangements, either as a parking garage with a small room in the rear, or as an open space to be divided and completed later on. Options were also offered for a variety of roof configurations to suit different urban settings (Friedman, 2001).

In this Montreal attached housing project, the architects selected roof angles that would permit use of the attic. The builder offered a dormer as a choice to occupants as part of a menu.

The moderately priced Grow Home was first built as a demonstration unit on the campus of McGill University in Montreal and was later adopted by local builders. Over 10,000 units have been built over the course of a decade by builders who offered an unfinished basement level to buyers. This strategy, along with other measures, helped lower the unit construction cost to $35,000. Over the years, buyers have chosen to adapt the space according to their particular needs. The variety of layouts conceived and built by the occupants themselves is a testament to the vitality of this strategy.

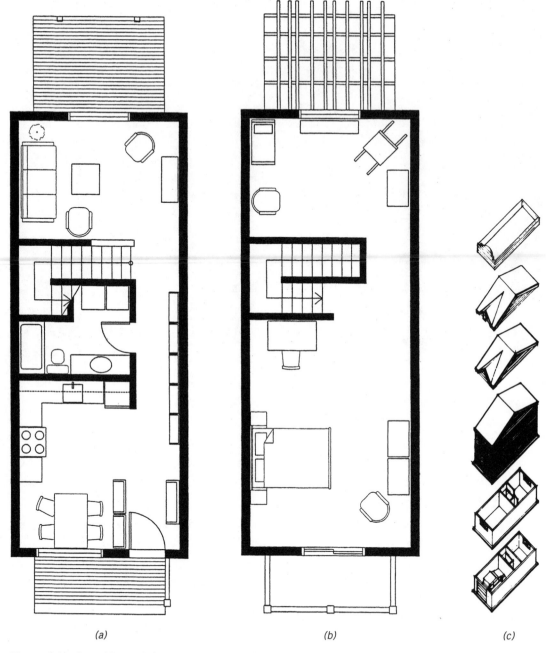

Plans of the Grow Home demonstration unit [(a) lower level and (b) upper level] with basement and roof options (c).

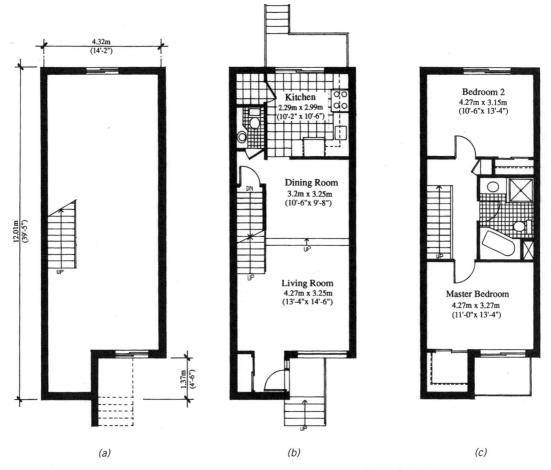

4.32m
(14'-2")

12.01m
(39'-5")

UP

1.37m
(4'-6")

Kitchen
2.29m x 2.99m
(10'-2" x 10'-6")

Dining Room
3.2m x 3.25m
(10'-6"x 9'-8")

DN

UP

UP

Living Room
4.27m x 3.25m
(13'-4"x 14'-6")

UP

Bedroom 2
4.27m x 3.15m
(10'-6"x 13'-4")

Master Bedroom
4.27m x 3.27m
(11'-0"x 13'-4")

UP

(a)   (b)   (c)

Modified Grow Home plans that were offered by builders to buyers. (a) Unfinished basement, (b) entrance level, and (c) upper level.

Basement levels of Grow Homes have been adapted by buyers to suit individual space needs.

Taking Advantage of Residual Spaces

Residual spaces are those that have been left over after space has been allocated for rooms and circulation. They are small areas that are found under stairs, as well as in alcoves of bay windows or corridors. They are valuable to a household since they can accommodate storage utilities needed for everyday items. This space is of even greater value in a small home where storage area is minimal. A well-thought-out design will ensure that these spaces are not randomly placed but are allocated to areas where storage is needed. As a result, the dimensions of these areas can be made to fit a cupboard when needed.

Storage cabinets have been placed in the bay window of this living room to take advantage of unused lower space. The top of the cupboards can be used as a seating arrangement.

From Single-Family to Two-Family

Division can take the form of converting a single-family dwelling into two units. The need may arise during the construction and marketing of the unit. When the development is zoned, for example, for single- or multifamily dwellings, the developer can offer both. A model unit is built, and decisions as to how to build the structure are made according to buyers' preferences and means. Conversion can also take place during the use of the home. When household size shrinks, the occupants can partition the space and create more than one dwelling, each with its own entry. A single-family unit will then become a duplex or triplex.

Several aspects need to be considered when such a strategy is followed. Attention must be paid to the location and the configuration of the entrance and its ability to accommodate entries to more than one dwelling. Acoustic performance will also have to be considered, with shared floors and walls insulated. Stacking plumbing lines will save on the future installation of a kitchen and bathroom in the new unit. The installation of an emergency means of egress to a separate upper dwelling unit is mandatory in many communities. Therefore, a staircase will have to be put in place for that purpose, likely in the rear.

These measures have been considered in the design of the Affordable Cottage. The home was conceived as a summer residence or as a permanent home for a small family. Since affordability was a concern, design strategies were introduced with cost-saving objectives in mind. Taking advantage of attic space was such a strategy. The upper level was turned into an independent unit with its own entrance. Once converted, the stairs leading to the second floor would be used by the occupant of the upper level only. In addition, the roof of the back porch was removed and a balcony installed with emergency stairs for the upper unit.

A Home Within a Home

When the need arises to accommodate an elderly member of the family, a portion of a home can be made into an independent dwelling. Intergenerational homes are common in several cultures, such as Japan and China. Married children there are expected to care for their elderly parents and to house

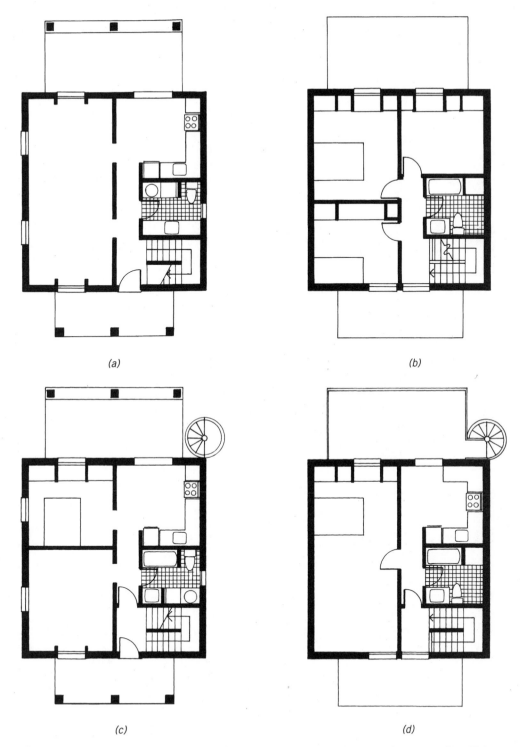

The Affordable Cottage was designed to facilitate conversion of a single-family dwelling [(a) first-stage ground level and (b) first-stage upper level] to a two-family structure [(c) converted ground level and (d) converted upper level].

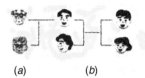

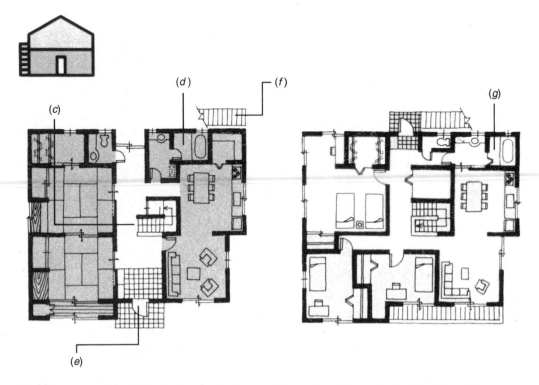

Manufacturers of prefabricated homes in Japan design a layout for extended families with a home within a home:

(a) Parents' household.

(b) Child's household.

(c) The interior staircase helps to create a sense of security since family members can help one another.

(d) The centralization of water pipes between the upper floor and the lower floor reduces the family's perception of the sound of running water.

(e) The entrance can be landscaped by locating a natural garden in front, which also gives the impression of a wider entrance.

(f) An exterior staircase allows the family to enter the second floor directly. The members of the child's household therefore do not bother the parents' household when returning home late at night.

(g) The plumbing is located in the corner to better serve both floors and to permit easy circulation for the occupants.

Unconverted   Ground floor   Second floor   Third floor

Converted   Ground floor   Second floor   Third floor

(a)

Unconverted   Ground floor   Second floor   Third floor

Converted   Ground floor   Second floor   Third floor

(b)

A variety of design options for sectioning an area to serve as a home within a home can be offered. (*a*) Townhouse with an integrated garage unit, (*b*) two-story house with a basement unit, (*c*) back-split house with a basement unit.

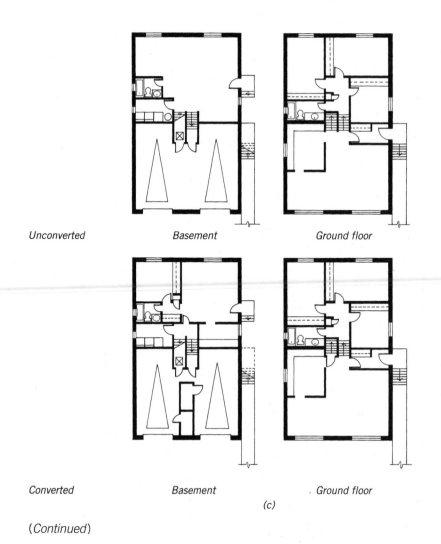

Unconverted   Basement   Ground floor

Converted   Basement   Ground floor

(c)

(*Continued*)

them. Sometimes when a new home is designed, a section of the space is made to function as an independent-dwelling unit. The design also foresees a situation where the sectioned area can later be restored to become part of the main space. The sectioned area can be on the lower floor of a three-story house in a space that would otherwise be made into a parking garage, a basement floor, or the back or side sections of the ground floor with its own independent unit.

TECHNOLOGY OF AND ACCESS TO UTILITIES

The introduction of new domestic technologies and building products has brought about a need to replace old ones. Wiring for computers, replacing cast-iron pipes with PVC plumbing, providing homes with more electricity to accommodate new, more powerful appliances, and as a result, changing entrance panels and wires are some of these changes. Changing utility conduits throughout the house is a possible yet costly, labor-intensive, and time-consuming task that often results in disruption to the occupants. The adaptable home, therefore, needs to permit such processes to take place easily and in a timely fashion.

The Need for a System Approach

During the life cycle of a home, the need to add, replace, or intervene with utilities occurs periodically. It could happen when a new technology or services such as wiring for television or computer use are introduced. At times, such as when new occupants move in, comprehensive work may take place. Remodeling a bathroom or kitchen, or completely overhauling the home's interior layout, are the type of undertakings that require a major change to utilities involving many systems.

The challenge to alterations resides in the way homes are constructed. Cables, pipes, ducts, or wires are installed on the periphery of a space. Whether in walls, floors, or ceilings, these conduits are passed through floor joists or wall studs, creating a network that ends up in a hub, usually in a mechanical room. The installation process itself takes place when the walls and the ceiling are exposed, without gypsum boards. Once installed, access to the wires themselves will require a reversal of the process: removing the wall or subfloor boards and exposing the conduits in order to manipulate them. It is no doubt a cumbersome procedure that modern building practices have attempted to change. Easy access to utilities requires a system approach to laying conduits. The system needs to allow the first or subsequent owners who wish to replace or upgrade subcomponents to locate them and carry out the work without interruptions to the occupants' daily lives.

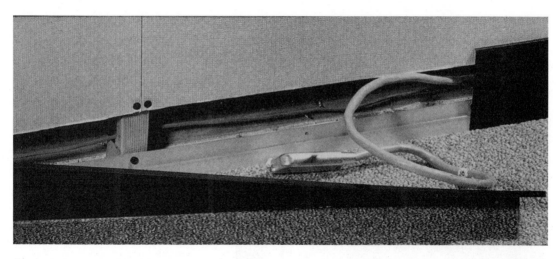

Common in commercial construction, a floor moulding panel in a partition permits easy access to wiring.

The practice of constructing for change is common in commercial structures. In office buildings, for example, where the occupants themselves or their requirements change frequently, installation of conduits and interior partitioning are made to allow ongoing modifications and rearrangements of the layout. The introduction of advanced computer technology or relocation of workstations often needs to be accomplished swiftly. Raised floors or suspended ceiling tiles permit a quick rerouting of ventilation pipes or the insertion of new computer cables. Similarly, partitions are designed to be dismantled and reinstalled elsewhere. Specially designed channels in these partition systems permit the easy fishing of cables through them. It is with this mind-set that a home needs to be designed and constructed. Technology that has been proven and accepted in commercial buildings can inspire the development of new products and residential construction practices.

Building a Chase

When simplified maintenance and the upgrade of utilities is sought, a method of laying them systematically needs to be established. The method, arranged hierarchically, aims to concentrate them in a single known location. From this location, they can branch out to different rooms in the house. The location of such a passageway, to be referred to here as a *chase,* can be in the floor, ceiling, or wall, or even in a combination of these locations.

In a wood-frame construction, a horizontal chase can be built in the floor along a perimeter wall or main circulation artery. It would contain the utility conduits, such as heating and cooling ducts, drains, and water supply. When upgrading or maintenance is required, a floor panel covering the chase would be removed. The panel, part of the subfloor, would be installed under a carpet or wood flooring.

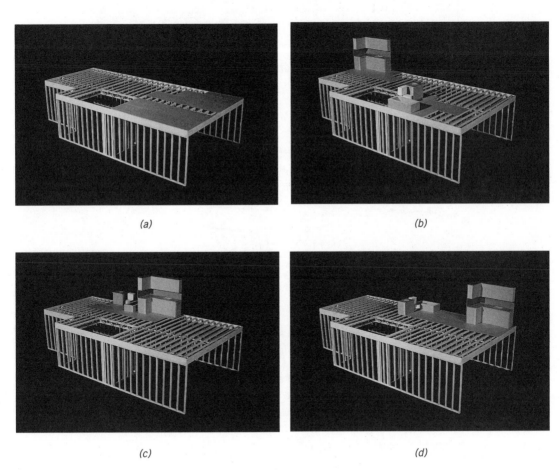

(a)

(b)

(c)

(d)

A floor chase in an open-web floor joist system (*a*) and alternative locations of wet functions on a floor [(*b*) through (*d*)].

(a)

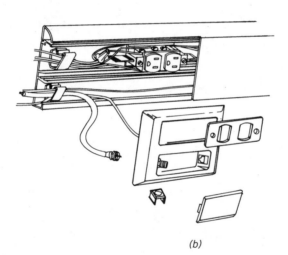

(b)

Photo of a baseboard raceway (*a*) and details of a jack (*b*). In response to the need to introduce and upgrade computers and telecommunication wires at home, the raceway was developed. The thrust of this product is that, for ease of manipulation, wire can be installed in a special device outside the wall. The system is made of a moulding that is placed along the perimeter at the base of the wall. The moulding conceals as well as organizes low-voltage cabling and electrical wiring. The system is a three-piece design, consisting of a base, snap-on cover, and snap-on trim. The base has channels for wiring that are separated by a barrier. Ribs located on the top channel are used for mounting device brackets. The cover of the system snaps onto the base with built-in flanges. The trim cover is fitted with tabs that serve to lock itself with the base and cover. Both the cover and trim cover are available in a wide range of finishes (e.g., PVC and wood veneers). The installation and upgrade of the system are also simplified by modular jacks and outlets.

The concentrated location and simplified access to utilities also widens the choice offered by builders to buyers at the preoccupancy stage. It increases the range of places in which a bathroom or kitchen can be located on a floor, thereby expanding the variability of possible layout configurations. Flexible hot- and cold-water pipes would be connected to the main supply pipes in the chase, and attention would also have to be paid to the length of the drainpipes as a sloping angle is required.

The building of such a chase is aided by several off-the-shelf building products. Open-web joists and flexible PVC pipes (described earlier), along with suspended ceiling tiles and wall-mounted raceways for electrical wires, are some of the devices that can provide easy access to utilities.

User Manual

The need to upgrade utilities requires familiarity with their unique method of installation, functioning, upkeep, and intervention. When the need to change a system arises, which may take place years after it was first installed, one needs to figure out how it all works. The system may be upgraded by a hired professional or by the homeowners themselves. The participation of homeowners often depends on how competent they are, how comfortable they are with facing technical challenges and handling tools.

A recent trend in the development of building products and tools has simplified the installation process for everyone. The realization that professional renovators need not be the only target of their marketing efforts has driven manufacturers to simplify design and instructions for use, and even lower the cost of many items. Their effort has been helped by an informal education process through television shows and how-to magazines. The need to provide a homeowner or hired professional with appropriate documentation that records the content of the home and enables them to intervene, upgrade, and repair it when necessary is paramount.

Other industries have recognized the need to familiarize their customers with common products. Along with a new car, a computer, or a motorized gardening tool, one finds a user manual that contains step-by-step installation instructions as well as upkeep advice. Some of the instructions are general, but many are specific to a particular model.

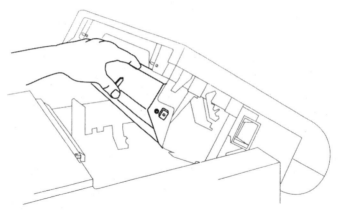

Figure 1-9
Inserting the toner cartridge

4. Loosen the tape tab.

Holding the cartridge in place, flex the black tab gently but firmly until it loosens. (See Figure 1-10.) Don't tear it completely away; you'll need it to pull out the sealing tape.

Figure 1-10
Flexing the black tab

Figure 1-11
Removing the tape from the toner cartridge

User manuals of products like computers provide detailed instructions for their installation and upkeep.

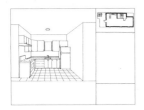

1. View of existing kitchen

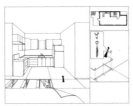

2. Remove floor covering and unscrew subfloor

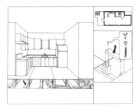

3. Dismantle joist bridge of plumbing chase

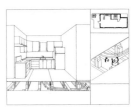

4. Disconnect drain pipes to sink

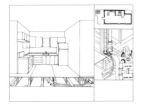

5. Disconnect main drain pipes in chase

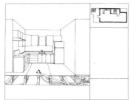

6. Remove disconnected drain pipe

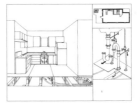

7. Disconnect kitchen sink drain pipes

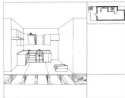

8. Disassemble kitchen

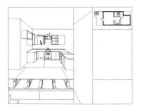

9. Reassemble kitchen in new location

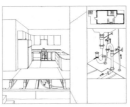

10. Connect drain pipe to sink

11. Place main drain pipe in chase

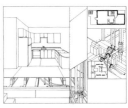

12. Connect main drain pipe to structure's drain

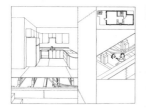

13. Connect sink drain to chase's drain

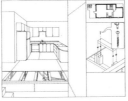

14. Place and screw the joist bridge

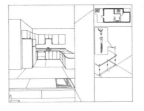

15. Screw back chase cover

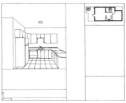

16. View of relocated kitchen

In an adaptable home, user manuals for a specific home may include step-by-step instructions on how to relocate a kitchen and, as a result, manipulate the plumbing.

Several North American housing authorities and publishers have authored generic manuals that provide guidance on the general maintenance and upkeep of homes. They illustrate how to clean rain gutters or provide instructions on how to check the foundation for cracks. What is missing, however, is a set of instructions for a particular sold model. Through drawings, which can be provided in a printed form or be part of the builder's website, homeowners will find the technical makeup of their homes. They will learn where exactly the conduits have been laid, how they can be accessed, what tools should be used, and once open, how they should be handled. Well-written and well-illustrated user manuals may deal with general upkeep as well as specific issues. An example of the latter would be the guided step-by-step instructions of how to relocate a kitchen from its original placement to another location in the house and, as a result, how to disconnect an extension to a drain pipe and refit flexible PVC pipes through open-web floor joists.

INTERIOR PREMANUFACTURED COMPONENTS

Interior prefabricated components are manufactured off-site and brought in for installation when the shell of a building is completed. They include bathroom fixtures, kitchen cabinets, storage files, and interior doors. Their method of production has evolved in recent years. The custom-designed portion of them has largely disappeared, and the share of man-made materials such as plastic or wood products has increased. They are likely to dominate the future construction practices of homes and also expand the choice given to buyers of new homes.

Buying a la Carte

The process of buying a new home in a tract development commonly begins with a visit to a site where a model home is inspected. Once the decision to buy has been made, the buyers will enter into negotiations on the price and the home's contents, which include a list of finishes and their respective qualities. It could include, for example, a choice of a kitchen that is made of oak or

All the parts to BILLY

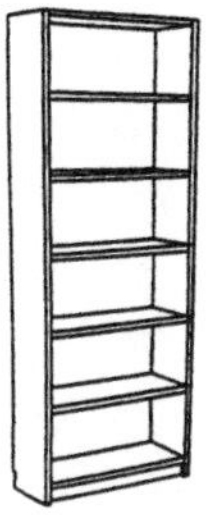

Bookcase
WxHxD
80x202x28 cm
31½x79½x11"
White $99
Oak $149
Red-brown $149
Pine $149
Birch $149
Beech $149
Black $149

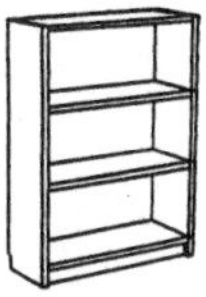

Bookcase
WxHxD
80x106x28 cm
31½x41¾x11"
White $79
Oak $99
Red-brown $99
Pine $99
Birch $99
Beech $99
Black $99

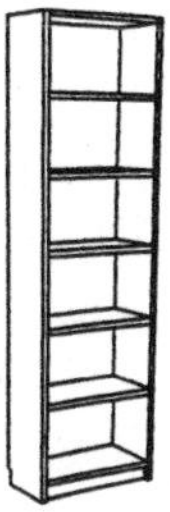

Bookcase
WxHxD
60x202x28 cm
23⅝x79½x11"
White $89
Oak $129
Red-brown $129
Pine $129
Birch $129
Beech $129
Black $129

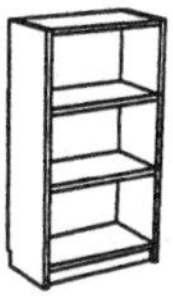

Bookcase
WxHxD
60x106x28 cm
23⅝x41¾x11"
White $69
Oak $89
Red-brown $89
Pine $89
Birch $89
Beech $89
Black $89

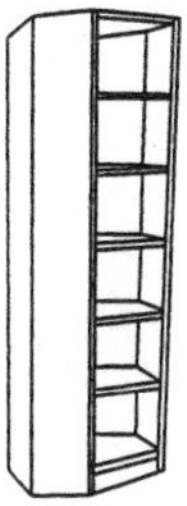

Corner bookcase
WxHxD
48x202x41 cm
17⅞x79½x16⅛"
White $190
Oak $250
Red-brown $250
Pine $250
Birch $250
Beech $250
Black $250

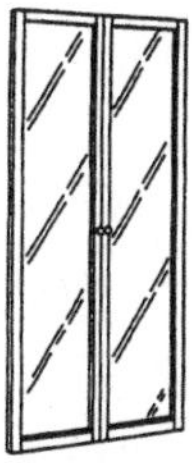

Pair of glass doors
WxH
80x194 cm
31½x76¾"
White $130
Oak $150
Red-brown $150
Pine $150
Birch $150
Beech $150
Black $150
Aluminium $170

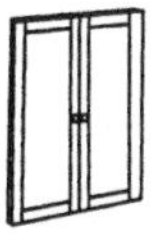

Pair of solid doors
WxH
80x98 cm
31x39"
White $80
Oak $90
Red-brown $90
Pine $90
Birch $90
Beech $90
Black $90

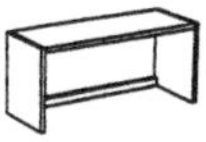

Height ext. unit
WxHxD
80x35x28 cm
31½x13⅝x11"
White $30
Oak $40
Red-brown $40
Pine $40
Birch $40
Beech $40
Black $40

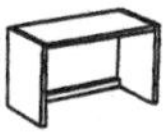

Height extension unit
WxHxD
60x35x28 cm
23⅝x13⅝x11"
White $25
Oak $35
Red-brown $35
Pine $35
Birch $35
Beech $35
Black $35

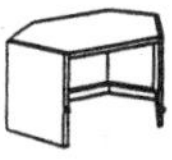

Corner height ext. unit
WxHxD
45x41x35 cm
17¾x16⅛x13¾"
White $40
Oak $50
Red-brown $50
Pine $50
Birch $50
Beech $50
Black $50

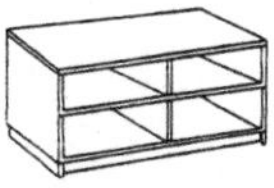

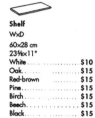

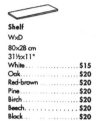

TV bench
WxHxD
90x50x50 cm
35⅜x19⅝x19⅝"
White $89
Oak $99
Red-brown $99
Pine $99
Birch $99
Beech $99
Black $99
Holds most 32" TVs.

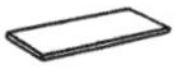

Shelf
WxD
60x28 cm
23⅝x11"
White $10
Oak $15
Red-brown $15
Pine $15
Birch $15
Beech $15
Black $15

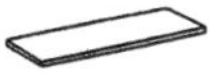

Shelf
WxD
80x28 cm
31½x11"
White $15
Oak $20
Red-brown $20
Pine $20
Birch $20
Beech $20
Black $20

Glass shelf 2-pack.
WxD
80 cm
31½" $15

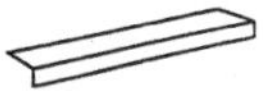

BILLY Bookcase lighting
56 cm, 22"
Brass $25.95
Black, white $25.95

76 cm, 29⅞"
Brass $35.95
Black, white $35.95

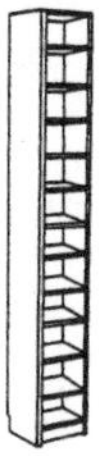

BENNO CD shelf
WxHxD
20x202x17 cm
7⅞x79½x6¾"
White $69
Oak $79
Red-brown $79
Pine $79
Birch $79
Beech $79
Black $79

A menu of options is offered by furniture manufacturers to buyers of this self-assembly unit.

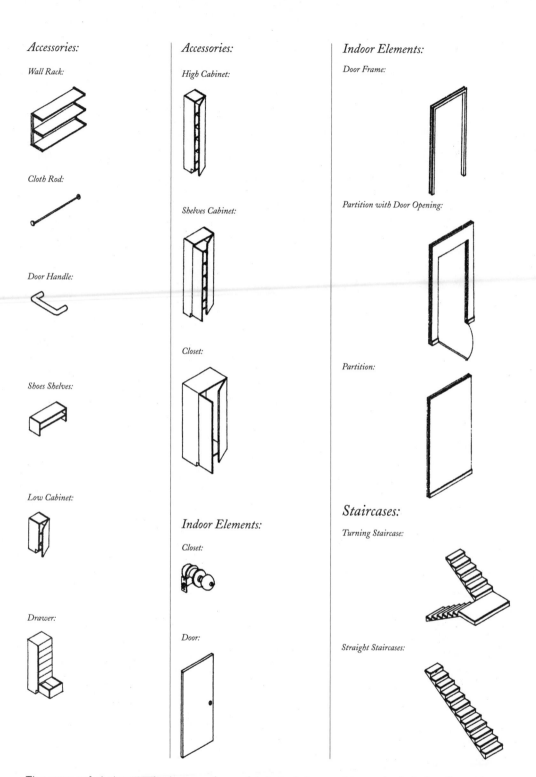

Accessories:

Wall Rack:

Cloth Rod:

Door Handle:

Shoes Shelves:

Low Cabinet:

Drawer:

Accessories:

High Cabinet:

Shelves Cabinet:

Closet:

Indoor Elements:

Closet:

Door:

Indoor Elements:

Door Frame:

Partition with Door Opening:

Partition:

Staircases:

Turning Staircase:

Straight Staircases:

The menu of choices to the buyers of a prefabricated, low-cost home included wall panels, stairs, doors, and storage cupboards.

melamine, a range of doors, or flooring quality. The decision as to what the choice package includes rests with the builder and his or her marketing team. This process is also common in other industries, such as the car industry, where some manufacturers offer variations on model types, colors, seat arrangement, or upholstery. Buyers of assemble-it-yourself furniture can, in some outlets, select from among the choices offered and purchase the parts that suit their budget and desired arrangement at home.

A similar mind-set can be applied to the design and selling of homes. Together with the designer, and after a careful study of the anticipated buyers, a menu of choices relevant to this particular group can be prepared. The menu, containing items and their costs, is displayed in the model unit for selection. It is commonly argued that to expand a choice in homes can result in confusion and indecision; therefore, only a limited number of suitably chosen options needs to be offered. Once selected, the items are fit into a unit layout by the occupants.

Demountable Walls

The menu of choices may also include walls. Similar to the current customary design and marketing of open-space lofts, a home can be sold as an open space with only a few rooms enclosed. The need to accommodate a variety of interior arrangements and to create a method whereby a buyer will be charged for the length of wall purchased is worthy of consideration, primarily at the low-cost end of the housing market. Another argument resides in the fact that removing partitions as the need arises is presently complicated by a building technique that, compared with European countries, is relatively flexible yet not simple to change. When relocation of walls takes place, it causes significant disruption to daily life.

Walls developed for use in office buildings offer easy installation and relocation. At present, the prefabricated walls are code-approved for commercial use; however, they still need to be made part of residential building codes in some jurisdictions. There are three types of demountable wall systems. The first is a *mobile* or *openable system,* which has a sliding mechanism that allows a wall panel to move along ceiling tracks. The second type is a *demountable system,* where the concept is similar in principle to that of a conventional drywall

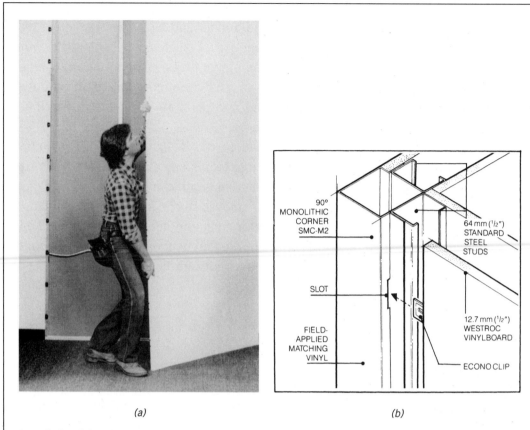

(a)   *(b)*

Installation (*a*) and details (*b*) of a demountable wall system. Some demountable partition system models are composed of a metal frame to which prefinished wallboards are affixed with special clips but without wet joints. The systems contain a ready-to-install prefabricated kit. The wall panels are held in place by a lock system, which eliminates the need to drill holes in a wood floor or to damage carpets. Punctured holes in the studs allow for wiring to be strung through them, increasing the system's flexibility. Alternatively, the manufacturer offers a horizontal wiring chase that is installed at the base of the wall. According to some manufacturers, installation costs are equivalent to a conventional wall. The monetary advantage, however, is in the ability to reuse the walls in other locations and also in the timesaving dismantling process.

system. The walls are constructed with metal studs that are placed at specific intervals. Prefinished wallboards are then affixed with special clips to the metal frame. The third type is the *portable partition system,* made of prefabricated panels, which are brought to a desired location and held in place by channels in the ceiling and floor.

Choosing and Placing

The increased share of prefabricated components in a home's interior provides the opportunity to view the design, construction, and purchasing of a home as an open-ended system. With the elimination of bearing partitions, the process can be seen as placing functions, the subcomponents that comprise them, and in the case of electrical appliances, plugging into an open shell. The approach widens the possible layout configurations and creates suitable conditions for a better match between households and their homes. It also contributes to a change of design practice and a transformation of the home delivery system.

From the current practice of specific floor plan design, the designer's role could become that of creating the conditions and the components necessary for choice. It would begin with the design of a structure, the shell and its openings, the placement of the main utility access to the shell, and the spread of the utilities throughout the structure. It would continue with the development of alternative layout configurations or space modules by the builder, to be selected by a buyer. The design of the subcomponents themselves could also become the role of the designer, moving from architectural to industrial design. Designers would also participate in accommodating the buyer in the purchase process of a home. They could act as facilitators in a choice process and would be responsible for ensuring that choices made in the interior coincide with the building's exterior design.

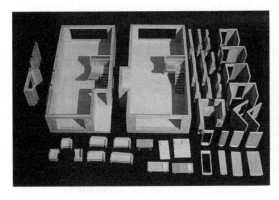 

The process of buying a home needs to include options offered to buyers who choose components that suit their space needs and budgets.

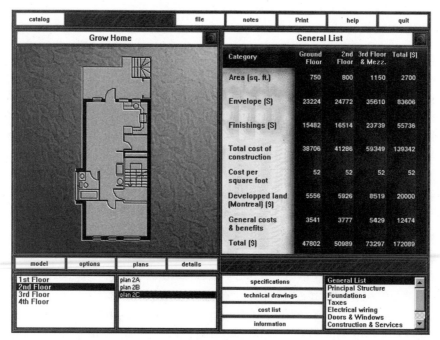

(a)

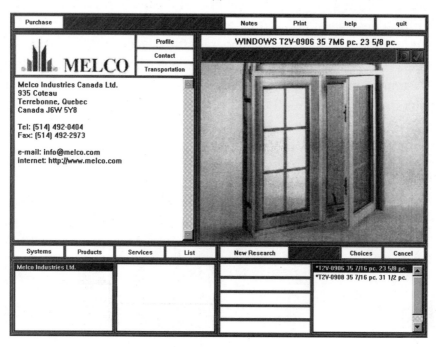

(b)

The use of computers simplifies the administration of the correlation between chosen components or home models and their cost. (*a*) Information on the chosen product, (*b*) relationship of cost to choices made.

Digital Tools

The design and choice processes of homes and their interiors have been assisted by advances in the field of computers. The ability to digitally display and store large amounts of information helps designers, builders, and buyers view design options and find out their costs. Once choices are made, computers facilitate the process of fitting them to the buyers' budgets. Software also helps to construct three-dimensional models of unbuilt homes, further illustrating what the results of the choices will look like. On a larger scale, computers are changing the traditional way of visiting a project location. Internet sites, set up by builders, let buyers visit projects from the comfort of their homes. They can view the project's site as well as the interior of a model home and select relevant items from a menu of choices offered before moving on to make up their minds and visit the location in person.

SURFACE FINISHES

Changes in construction practices and the introduction of products that permit a distinction between the building's structure and its interior have also led to new opportunities in surface finishes. After the rough construction of the home has been completed and the interior partitions and ceiling have been clad with gypsum boards, the time to cover them arrives. Surface finishes contribute to the final look of the home. Along with furnishings, they make the house cozy, warm, or cold. They include a range of products for floor coverings, such as linoleum, ceramic tiles, parquet wood tiles, or wall-to-wall carpeting. The walls are also covered with wallboard, tiles, or simply painted.

The choice of how they want their homes to be finished is made by buyers at the time of design or, in tract developments, at the model home during purchase. The buyers evaluate their options and try to personalize their newly acquired homes. There are also cost implications. Natural oak-strip wood flooring will cost more than wall-to-wall carpeting. There will also be maintenance implications. Some coverings such as carpets have to be washed periodically. Buyers with limited budgets will choose less expensive products, with the possibility in mind of upgrading them later.

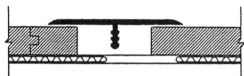

(a)   (b)

Image and details of floating floors. (*a*) Photo of a floating floor, (*b*) diagram of an expansion joint. One of the distinguishing features of a floating floor which makes it different from conventional wood floors is not being attached to the subfloor. It is held in place by tongue-and-groove, which makes installation quick and cost-effective. The flooring is made of high-density, moisture-resistant fiberboard panels. These panels are composed of wood residues such as sawdust, wood chips, and shavings from processing factories. The ligneous material is ground into a pulp to which a resin is added. This pulp is then dried and pressed into panels of specific density which, depending on the product, is greater than 50 or 55 pounds per cubic foot (0.64 to 0.71 kilograms per cubic meter), which makes the floor highly durable. The first layer is a protective coating that provides a wear-resistant surface. The second layer is a decorative surface that comes in a wide selection of design options. The third layer is the HDF panel, which is wood-based and precision-engineered for quality and strength. Its tongue-and-groove system provides a snug fit for a perfect finish. The last layer, called the balancing layer, provides dimensional stability and a moisture barrier for added protection that also permits floor washing.

The range of offerings to buyers would be determined by the builder. Commonly, a standard package of finishes would be included with the home's price. There would be a range of colors and patterns for flooring or wall coverings. Then there will be additional, higher-quality products that, if selected, would cost more than the standard package. Known as *extras,* these products would have to be ordered specially or would require specialized application.

Simpler Installation

Ongoing innovation and the introduction of new composite materials provide greater opportunities for choice and adaptability in homes. The use of plastics and fiberboard allows easy installation and the replacement of surface products when needed. The principal nature of these products is in not being part of the surface to which they are affixed, and in the fact that their installation process permits easy removal. The installation of wall or floor tiles is made with ready-to-apply bonding materials, which, unlike in the past, do not require mixing. Plastic sheeting placed under the tiles prevents leakage through them but also facilitates their removal.

When ceramic tiles are beyond the budget of a homeowner, other materials are available. Seamless plastic sheets are available to replace wall tiles around the bathtub, and sheets of linoleum in trendy colors are offered as replacements for floor coverings. Among the choices offered to home buyers for floors are high-density fiberboards. Their advantage is not only in their low cost but also in the choice of patterns and the ability to remove and replace them easily.

The projects selected for presentation here were all designed with adaptability in mind. The common thread that runs through them is their response to societal challenges. Demographic shifts that have given rise to new household compositions, the aging of the population, the need to build sustainable communities and densify urban environments, and the conservation of natural resources are some of the key features addressed by these projects. In light of these issues, the projects integrate new technologies in an effort to lower cost and increase the level of choice and adaptability offered to occupants. The homes, designed by the author and his team, are to a certain degree variations on the seed concept of an adaptable multistory structure. Each design, however, was conceived with a different programmatic objective in mind.

THE NEXT HOME

The Next Home was designed and constructed as a demonstration unit on the campus of McGill University in Montreal, Canada (Friedman et al. 1996). The home was conceived after a process of inquiry into societal changes, techno-logical innovations, and environmental concerns. The fundamental conclusion of this thought process was that accelerated demographic and lifestyle changes required an open-ended approach to home design. This approach could mani-fest itself in greater choice during the buying process and adaptability through-out the residency.

Another aspect highlighted in the design of the Next Home is recognition of the factors and forces that influence the North American home building indus-try. While the home was designed to be built using methods of construction familiar to the industry, the design nonetheless contains a variety of innovations in the way process or products are used and assembled.

Affordability was another consideration. The Next Home was designed to be sold and fitted out according to the space needs and the budget of the occu-pants. It was also meant to demonstrate that future designers will have to place environmental considerations high on their priority list. Attention was therefore paid to the selection of materials that reduce reliance on natural resources and that increase the home's energy performance.

Urban Configuration

At the outset of the Next Home's design, a comprehensive scenario was con-structed in which the urban setting was a key part. Because of its dimensions and inherent adaptability, the home was designed to be built in infill sites as well as new tract developments. Here, too, we introduced a new perspective that not only contributes to the creation of a pleasant urban environment but also supports sustainable living. The design was also meant to demonstrate that adaptability can support another objective with far-reaching societal implica-tions: the reduction of urban sprawl. In recent decades, it has become evident that present planning and community development practices have had negative ramifications for the environment. Urban sprawl has contributed to the exten-sive use of the car and, as a result, to increased gas emissions. It has also necessitated the construction of highways to support local and long-distance commuting, which has left its imprint on the landscape.

The single-family detached home was a common housing solution when the majority of households had a similar demographic background. However, societal changes have given rise to a wide range of households, some of which do not want to reside in single-family detached homes or in apartment buildings. The Next Home was meant to provide an in-between alternative. It was designed to be a ground-related prototype with higher-density attributes, yet not to be regarded as a walk-up apartment building.

Increased-density communities pose design challenges, one of which is the need to accommodate a higher number of dwelling units—and, as a result, more cars. Providing appropriate private and public green spaces is another challenge. Tract developments with high-density housing may also lead to extensive architectural repetition and a loss of identity for a cluster of houses or a building. The need to respond to these challenges was paramount in conceiving the urban applications of the Next Home.

Detached, Semidetached, or Row House?

The common approach to the design of housing developments is to create a limited number of housing prototypes. Such an approach is often mandated by zoning regulations legislated by the municipality. Often only one type of dwelling—single detached, semidetached, or row—is constructed.

In the design of the Next Home, it was argued that a variety of housing prototypes within the same development had to be offered. A mix of homes would contribute to the creation of a variety of household types as well as a wider price range. A traditional family could purchase an entire stand-alone structure, while another home buyer searching for a more affordable housing solution could look for a single unit—a floor within a similar structure.

In order to allow for such variation to occur, a suitable dwelling proportion needed to be used. As indicated earlier, 20 feet (6.1 meters) wide × 35 feet (10.7 meters) tall would provide a suitable proportion for a structure to stand alone or to be part of a semidetached house or a row. This measure of adaptability provides an opportunity for a wide range of urban configurations and planning arrangements. It also requires a coherent urban design approach concerning the placement of each type in the development.

The chosen proportions of the Next Home enabled planners and builders to build the structure as a detached or semi-detached dwelling, or as part of a row. The model shows the front elevation of such configurations.

Mixed Uses and Mixed Users

One of the hallmarks of current urban development is the segregation of uses. Zoning regulations often mandate the separation of commercial and residential activities, which does not foster sustainable living and increases reliance on motor vehicles. The Next Home was designed to accommodate, either on or above the ground floor, commercial uses, ranging from a home office to a small service business like a travel agency or medical clinic. In order to accommodate such activities, the main entry door is recessed to allow direct access from the outside to the lower level without requiring use of the structure's main door. This provides privacy for the occupants of the lower and upper levels and enables the occupants of the lower commercial use to link the space to the floor above by internal stairs, avoiding the need to step outside.

A community of Next Homes was designed to integrate a variety of prototypes within the same development.

In a traditional urban setting, commercial use is mixed with residential.

Adaptable Parking

The motor vehicle is part of urban reality in North American communities. Circulation within developments and, in particular, parking are therefore a critical concern of planners of higher-density settings, including designers of Next Home projects. Parking of 18 to 24 units per acre (45 to 60 per hectare) can account for nearly 50 percent of total site area. It is therefore vital to approach the design of parking with the same mind-set used in arranging the grouping of homes.

Surface parking, as opposed to indoor parking, is considered by many to be unattractive yet more affordable. Parking in front of units is a low-cost solution—eliminating the need for construction of an alley—but it requires a 15- to 20-foot (4.6- to 6.1-meter) setback, distancing any potential commercial activities from the street. Side parking preserves the backyard but erodes cohesion of the street face by creating large gaps between buildings (40 to 60 feet [12.2 to 18.3 meters]) if the driveway is shared. This form of parking is appropriate for cluster scenarios where street alignment is not a priority. Parking in the rear requires alley access but provides a continuous street face and a minimum setback, encouraging maximum density at the lowest cost and permitting flexibility of use for ground-level units. Alley access to backyards through the center of the block provides a high degree of flexibility at a relatively low cost, and it gives the occupants of a single structure greater control than any centralized parking scenario. The key to rear alley access is the provision of lot and block sizes of sufficient depth to allow both garden space (a green buffer) and parking.

Indoor parking can be accommodated either at grade or below grade. At-grade parking is viable with front and side options within a structure as well as in a common back garage. Below-grade parking, while preserving the ground-floor unit, separates the unit from the street in height and/or setback, thereby reducing the viability of commercial activities and handicapped accessibility. Garage parking within the structure hides the car and preserves the backyard, but it reduces the area of the ground-floor unit and requires a setback from the street to accommodate the grade change if located below grade. The most adaptable option is to design at-grade ground-floor space that can be modified from garage to commercial/residential and vice versa. Side parking allows the maximum number of cars within the structure, preserves the commercial/residential unit at grade in the adjacent structure (if shared) as well as the backyard, and allows two optional surface parking spaces at the end of the driveway. This form of parking requires 20 feet (6.1 meters) between semidetached buildings, an 80-square-foot (8-square-meter) driveway, and structural reinforcement of the side wall. Side parking is feasible for row houses at the end of the row and can accommodate up to four cars in a freestanding unit scenario. A carport, as an extension of an individual structure, allows for enclosed parking without adding a basement or occupying ground-floor space, and the backyard can be accessed without penetrating the dwelling. The disadvantage of this form of parking is that the increased livable area above the carport reduces the affordability of each unit. A setback must be incorporated to reduce the overall increase in area and the facade must be modified.

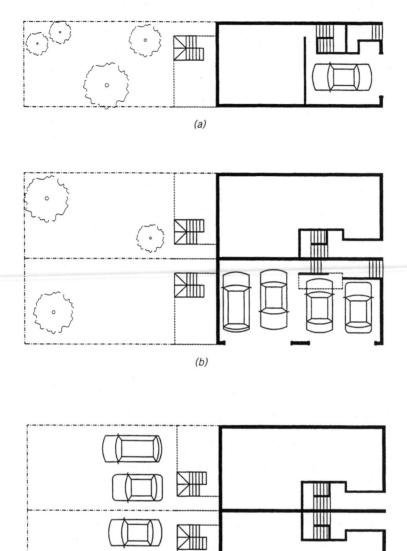

(a)

(b)

(c)

Typical parking alternatives in a Next Home community include indoor parking arrangements (a) and (b) and an outdoor parking arrangement with access to an alley (c).

The Built Environment

The variety of design configurations just outlined offers other opportunities. When the structures are assembled together to form clusters, the element of human scale is introduced. Height then becomes an important aspect when related to the open spaces around which the buildings are constructed. The chosen height and prototype will be selected based on market demand and a preconceived master plan that takes zoning regulations into consideration. Three-story structures can be placed around wider open spaces, and low-rise structures—perhaps two stories—around more confined areas.

Public open spaces are essential in a Next Home community because the amount of green area allocated to each unit is significantly reduced. It is desirable to plan the development in such a way that each dwelling has a view to an open space and ground-floor levels have direct access to it through a private backyard.

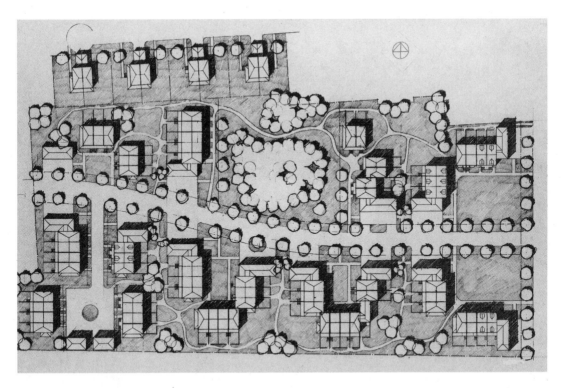

In higher-density Next Home communities, the grouping of the units emphasizes the creation of open spaces accessible to all.

Buy by the Floor

Demographic and lifestyle diversity, which influences home buyers' search for a dwelling, has shaped an additional feature of the Next Home: its volumetric configuration. It has been recognized that the rise in the number of nontraditional households has created a need to house a range of family types. As a result, the three-story structure can house a single family that occupies all floors, become a home to two families, or be a triplex housing three families. The marketing process for the Next Home will be part of a scenario whereby the units are sold according to home buyer demand. It is likely that in a loca-

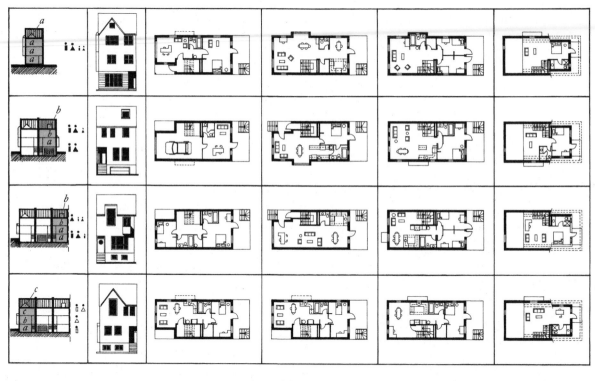

| Household and volumetric configuration | Front elevation | Ground floor | Second floor | Third floor | Mezzanine |

One of the features of the Next Home is the option extended to buyers to purchase the type and size of house that they need and can afford. The three-story structure can be sold as a single-family house, a duplex, or a triplex.

tion where there is a concentration of smaller households, a larger number of structures will be divided into triplexes and duplexes rather than being sold as single-family units.

In order for such adaptability to occur, a footprint of 20 × 40 feet (6.1 × 12.2 meters) was selected. The 800-square-foot (80-square-meter) area of each floor allows it to function as a self-contained one- or two-bedroom apartment. Buyers of two-story units would therefore have dwellings with a total area of 1600 square feet (160 square meters).

Entering the Next Home

Access and circulation are crucial to achieving adaptability in the Next Home. In addition to flexibility in arranging the volumetric configuration of the structure, it can be built below or on grade. The level below grade, a basement, can be habitable or can serve as a garage.

The stairs are another element that facilitates the structure's adaptability. Similar to the design of a walk-up apartment building, a single staircase serves all floors. These may be public stairs used by all three households in a triplex, or private stairs in a single-family arrangement. Placing the stairs along the longitudinal wall allows the area of each floor to be left open to accommodate a variety of interior layout arrangements. In addition recessing the stairs enables the front end of the unit to be better used and allows accommodation of an independent function, such as a home office, with its own entry.

Adding In and Adding On

The Next Home was designed to provide an opportunity for growth and division throughout its life cycle. It was viewed as a structure in which ongoing change would occur along with the lives of its inhabitants. Two scales of growth were envisioned. The first involved minor transformations that would take place within the unit—for example, combining two rooms to make a single space— and the second included changes that would alter the volumetric arrangement of the structure—the configuration of its floors. As well, additions to the exterior of the structure are offered. The add-on expansion that would take place during the buying process or the occupancy would be based on a prepared menu of options, outlined in the following text.

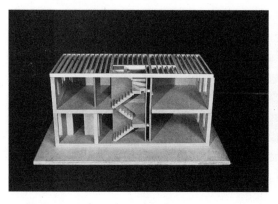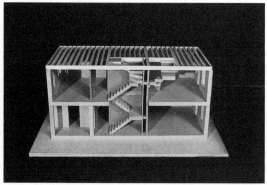

The joists between the levels have been prepared for easy removal and the installation of internal stairs in order to join floors.

As this study model demonstrates, the Next Home was designed to accommodate add-on expansions in the rear.

In order to facilitate the process of joining floors, a study was conducted of the possible locations for the introduction of internal stairs. It was recognized that a suitable location would be behind the structure's main stair shaft. As a result, the joists in that location were arranged to permit their easy removal so that conventional or prefabricated stairs could be built there. It was also envisioned that an add-on expansion in the form of a room might be made to the unit either during the buying process or the occupancy.

In order to make sure that additions fit in with the overall character of the cluster or the neighborhood, design guidelines must be created for a new development and submitted for approval along with a master plan.

The Next Home Facades

The recognition that the Next Home would be built in a community of such homes, and often in rows, initiated a need to pay attention to the diversity of facade design. Facade appearance is commonly influenced by the building's style, the urban context in which it is built, and zoning regulations. Therefore a method had to be proposed that would take into consideration these aspects as well as the fact that the Next Home would be a single- or multifamily building.

In general, it was envisioned that two levels of intervention would take place, the first of which would occur when the designer and builder decided on the overall configuration of the structure and its cladding materials. The number of floors, the articulation of the roof, and the types of windows would have to be agreed upon. Based on initial decisions, guidelines would be formulated. The guidelines for the Next Home are in the form of opening zones—areas in which infill components (windows or doors) are inserted.

The subsequent stage in the design of the Next Home's facades involved the creation of a menu of exterior elements, which would be shown to the builder to assist in the design of the facade. A smaller number of elements would then be selected and offered to home buyers. This would not only accommodate the desire to personalize but to relate decisions about the home's interior and the exterior openings. For example, a larger window might be required for a room that would serve as a home office.

The menu of exterior elements would also contain infill facade components, roof design variations, and dormer types. Add-on elements such as entire

Windows	($)	Roof Variations	($)	Add-on Elements	($)
305mm x 305mm (2' x 2')	170	Flat Roof:	8463	Backyard Patio:	$569
305mm x 610mm (2' x 4')	220	Pitched Roof with metal roofing: with asphalt shingles:	4146 3422	Rear Balcony (includes staircase):	1539
610mm x 610mm (4' x 4')	385	Pitched Roof with metal roofing: with asphalt shingles:	4146 3422	Balcony Enclosure:	3852
		Pitched Roof with metal roofing: with asphalt shingles:	5292 4426	Pergola:	410

Exterior Finishes

Front Facade		Large Rear Dormer:		One-story Bay Window	
Brick:	4050	with windows and door:	9177	metal roofing:	1197
Stucco:	3500	without windows and door:	8342	asphalt shingles:	1165
Vinyl Siding:	810				
Wood Siding:	1080				
Rear Facade		Front Dormer			
Brick:	4800	metal roofing:	591		
Stucco:	4148	asphalt shingles:	532		
Vinyl Siding:	960				
Wood Siding:	1280				
Side Facade				Two-story Bay Window	
Brick:	7800			metal roofing:	2327
Stucco:	6738	Front Dormer		asphalt shingles:	2295
Vinyl Siding:	1560	(including window):	1244		
Wood Siding:	2080				

Menu of exterior elements for the Next Home demonstration unit. The menu was prepared by the designer for the benefit of the builder and home buyers. (Prices are in Canadian dollars.)

Facade studies based on previously established opening zones and infill components.

rooms, balconies, and bays would be shown as well. Once an element was selected, its cost would be added to the overall cost of the base model.

Constructing the Next Home

When the conception of the Next Home ended, the preparation for its construction began. Since the modular nature of the design made it appropriate for prefabrication, the plans were handed to a prefabricator for translation into industrialized production. The dimensions of the structure made panelization the most suitable and adaptable method of manufacturing.

The assembly process of the Next Home was meant to follow the same mind-set as the design itself. The enclosure and its structural components were

(a)

(b) *(c)*

Front (a), side (b), and rear (c) elevations of the Next Home demonstration unit.

1.	2.	3.
4.	5.	6.
7.	8.	9.

Sequence of on-site structural assembly of the Next Home.

Fabrication of panels

Constructing the foundation and first floor

First-floor panel

Prefabricated roof trusses

Applying stucco to the exterior

Installing plumbing fixtures

Wiring the structure

Drywall and plaster

Tiling the bathrooms

Painting

Installing floating floors

Assembling kitchen cabinets

Construction process of the Next Home.

built first, followed by internal fittings independent of the structure that would be selected by home buyers. This approach let the builder introduce changes and accommodate variable market demand and clients' needs after construction began.

A closed system was selected from among the panelized methods available. Once the structure of a panel was constructed, windows and doors were installed and the panel was insulated with a product made of recycled paper. The outer skin of the panel was constructed of modular cement boards. The panels were then delivered to the campus for assembly. Special hooks placed in the panels during fabrication were used to hoist them into place and affix them to the floors.

Prefabrication of a sort was also used in the assembly of the Next Home's floors. Open-metal-web joists were laid on top of the exterior panels, plywood boards were nailed to the tops of the joists, and the next floor's exterior panels were placed on top of them. The open-web joists were designed and placed to contain a horizontal utilities chase in which the main conduits were located. Since the demonstration unit was meant to be on display for a limited time, the chase was left empty. Once the structure was completed, construction of the interior began. This process of fitting included installation of prefabricated interior partitions, plumbing fixtures, and then finishings.

Selling the Next Home

The Next Home could be built as a single structure on an infill lot or as part of a new tract housing development. It was envisioned that a master plan would be prepared, showing roads, parking, private and public open spaces, and a variety of dwelling configurations arranged as rows, semidetached, or stand-alone structures. Once a project was approved by a municipality, the marketing and construction process would begin. Advertisements would draw visitors to a sales office or model home.

The buying process would involve selecting from among a variety of offered options, beginning with buyers deciding where in the project (or a phase of it) they wished to reside, which building configuration they wanted. Prices would vary for each of these options.

Based on budget, home buyers would decide on the number of floors they wanted to buy. In the sales office there would be a display of standard options

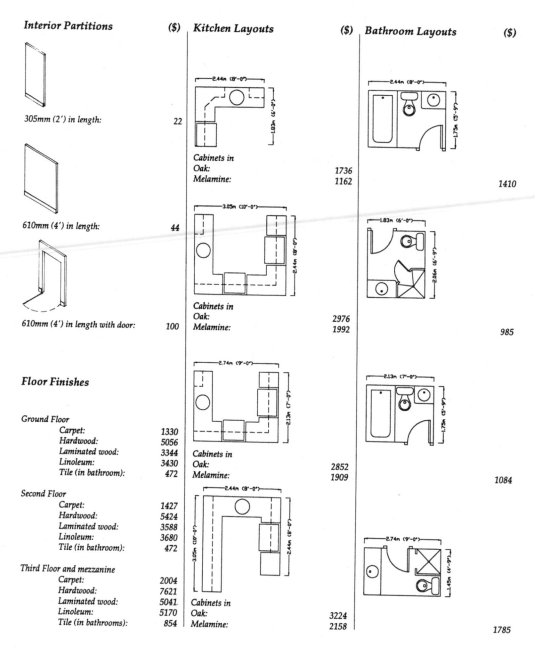

Interior Partitions	($)	Kitchen Layouts	($)	Bathroom Layouts	($)

Interior Partitions

305mm (2') in length: 22

610mm (4') in length: 44

610mm (4') in length with door: 100

Floor Finishes

Ground Floor
Carpet: 1330
Hardwood: 5056
Laminated wood: 3344
Linoleum: 3430
Tile (in bathroom): 472

Second Floor
Carpet: 1427
Hardwood: 5424
Laminated wood: 3588
Linoleum: 3680
Tile (in bathroom): 472

Third Floor and mezzanine
Carpet: 2004
Hardwood: 7621
Laminated wood: 5041
Linoleum: 5170
Tile (in bathrooms): 854

Kitchen Layouts

Cabinets in
Oak: 1736
Melamine: 1162

Cabinets in
Oak: 2976
Melamine: 1992

Cabinets in
Oak: 2852
Melamine: 1909

Cabinets in
Oak: 3224
Melamine: 2158

Bathroom Layouts

1410

985

1084

1785

Menu of interior elements prepared for the Next Home demonstration unit. (Prices are in Canadian dollars.)

and their prices. The marketing director would fit the choices made to the available unit. Based on anticipated household composition at a given location, some units would be designated as triplexes, others as duplexes, and some as single-family homes. There could be special cases, such as an extended family buying an entire structure and arranging it as a duplex with the elders occupying the ground floor, or a home buyer purchasing an entire structure, setting up an office on the ground floor, and living above it.

Once the location of the unit and the number of floors were selected, attention would be paid to the exterior and interior options. A home buyer could choose to purchase a balcony or pergola, or a lower-floor occupant could have a deck installed in the rear. Each option would have a specified price. The offerings would be prepared by the designer and the builder and would also fit in with a design code for the entire community.

Interior options would be selected next, following two levels of decision making. First-level decisions would relate to the spatial configuration of the entire unit. Buyers could select a predesigned layout or participate with the designer in an interior arrangement most suitable to their lifestyle. For example, they would have a choice of bathrooms and kitchens, which they would be able to place anywhere on a given floor. Those who purchased an open-concept design without interior walls would receive a financial credit. The second decision-making level would deal with interior finishings. Selections of wall and floor coverings, as well as styles and materials for doors and cabinetry, would be made by buyers at this stage. Once again, the buyers could decide to acquire a prepared package of finishings or go through a selection process that suited their budget.

The process described here was, to a large extent, modeled after the traditional marketing of North American housing developments. It has been expanded to include more options and alternatives to suit a wide range of home buyers. It is also expected that in the sales office of a Next Home project, computers will facilitate the selection process and offer a virtual walk through the unbuilt spaces.

Construction Scenarios

In order to illustrate choices available to buyers of the Next Home demonstration unit, a scenario was prepared for the entire structure and for each floor. Part of a row of on-grade homes was constructed. Based on the antici-pated composition of home buyers at the site's location, the developer decided to sell the structure as a triplex. Three households would therefore occupy the unit. Following is a fictitious scenario for each household's back-ground, motive for purchase, and rationale for decisions made about exterior and interior choices.

Mike's Place: Ground Floor

Mike, the owner of the ground-floor unit, is a 62-year-old widower retired after a long career as a civil servant. He decided to sell the big home that he and his wife had shared in a suburban location, where they raised two children who have since left home. Mike purchased the Next Home unit because the project was centrally located and because he did not want to burden his retirement income with high maintenance costs. After he sold his large home and pur-chased the unit, he invested the remaining amount in order to supplement his earnings. He also decided to take advantage of his career experience and allo-cate a portion of his newly acquired home for an office where he would operate a small consulting business. He selected the ground-floor unit because it would ensure accessibility as he got older.

The major feature of the ground-floor unit's design is the combination of an office and home environment. Mike chose to locate his kitchen and laundry area

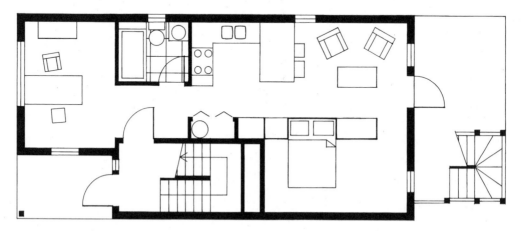

The owner of the ground-floor unit, a 62-year-old widower, decided to have an open concept. He located a home office in the front of the unit.

centrally, opposite the main entrance, thereby separating the private zone in the rear (living/dining area and bedroom) from the public zone (home office) in the front. The home office, which can be accessed from inside the unit through the foyer adjacent to the main entrance, can also be entered directly from the outside porch. In order to let more sunlight into the office, Mike, together with the designer, selected a larger window for the front. When Mike retires from his business activities, the office can be transformed into a bedroom or living room.

There are very few interior walls in this ground-floor unit: with the exception of the bathroom walls and the wall at the entrance to the office, storage units serve as dividers between spaces. This open concept also contributed to lower-

The front home office

The kitchen/dining area

The living space with exit to back patio

The bedroom space

Views of the ground-floor unit's interior.

ing the cost of Mike's unit. To maximize the living area in the rear of the unit, Mike has chosen to position his dining table directly adjacent to the kitchen counter; he retains the option of moving the table into the living area when he must accommodate a larger number of diners. The kitchen, much like the rest of the unit, was designed to accommodate the needs of a person using a wheelchair, as Mike sees himself aging in place and living an independent life as long as possible. Also, the walls in the full bathroom, placed near the entrance to be used by visitors as well, have plywood installed in them to simplify the attachment of grab bars when needed. The washer and dryer are in the kitchen zone, stacked to save space. The backyard and patio behind the unit are accessed through a door in the living room to allow Mike to pursue his outdoor hobbies with ease.

Jennifer and Mark's Place: The Second-Floor Unit

The occupants of the second-floor unit are a young couple without children who have been married for three years. Mark, age 27, is a computer software consultant who has been employed with a firm for under a year and a half. Jennifer, age 25, works full time as sales director for a chain of stationery stores. She also attends evening classes at a local university in pursuit of an MBA degree. Until they purchased their Next Home unit, Jennifer and Mark rented a two-bedroom

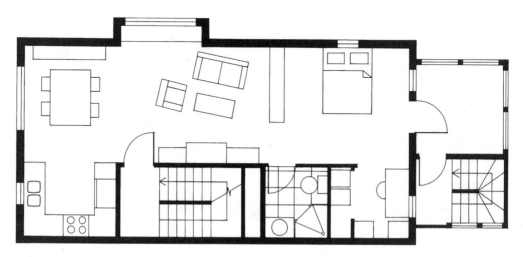

Floor plan of Jennifer and Mark's place on the second floor of the Next Home.

flat in an apartment building. The fact that their rent was approximately equal to the mortgage for their own Next Home unit convinced them to purchase. Since they did not see themselves expanding their family in the immediate future, they decided to buy an apartment rather than a single-family detached home. Their limited budget was a main concern. The ability to pick and choose and to buy only the items they needed was therefore a key factor in enabling them to buy in a Next Home project.

The spatial configuration of Jennifer and Mark's floor is that of an open concept. In fact, they purchased a large open space. The private zone is located in the rear and the public zone in the front, and furniture is used to divide the

Kitchen

Living and dining area

Bedroom

Multipurpose room

Views of the second floor unit's interior.

home. Unlike Mike downstairs, Jennifer and Mark located their kitchen against the common wall of the row. A tight budget led them to purchase lower kitchen cabinets only, with metal shelves purchased at a local furniture store installed for dish storage. In consultation with the project's designer, Jennifer and Mark placed the sink against the front wall, where a single long, narrow window was constructed.

After closely examining a menu of choices offered to them by the builder, Jennifer and Mark decided to buy a bathroom with a shower in order to accommodate their desire for a study space. They decided to locate the study space in the rear, where a window would provide a view to the back. The space consolidates three different activities: side-by-side washer and dryer, clothing storage in self-assembled cabinets, and a work station. They envisioned that they might one day turn this space into a room with its own door with built partitions.

Reflection on their future space needs led Jennifer and Mark to purchase an add-on room in the rear. The couple selected this feature from a menu of exterior offerings, along with a bay window, and decided to use it as an enclosed balcony for storage at first. They saw themselves finishing the add-on by themselves, creating another full-fledged room.

Boards made of high-density fiber (HDF) were selected for the floor covering. The boards, also referred to as *floating floors,* were laid atop a thin sheet of foam placed above the plywood. Jennifer and Mark accented the edges of the floor with a border made of a different shade of the same material. In order to define the spaces, they consulted a color chart and selected a bright color. Storage cabinets were placed under the window in the bay, and their tops became a seating area. All the conduits for computer and telephone cables and electrical and telephone wires were placed in a raceway that runs around the entire perimeter of the unit, providing the couple with the flexibility to place a receptacle wherever they wished and to change the placement throughout their residency.

Susan, Lisa, and Eric's Place: The Third-Floor-and-Mezzanine Unit

The raising of the roof in the back part of the Next Home structure provided an opportunity to offer a mezzanine to the buyer of the third floor. The buyer of these two levels was Susan, the 41-year-old single mother of 14-year-old Lisa and 11-year-old Eric. Susan liked the idea of turning the upper level into her own space where she would have a study, a second living room, and a bedroom

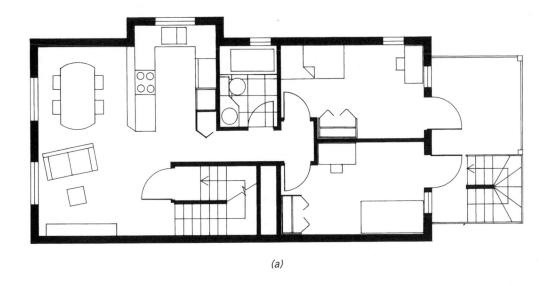

(a)

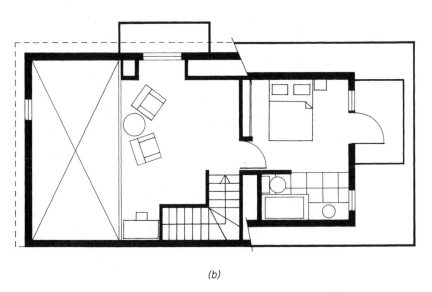

(b)

Floor plans of the Next Home's third floor (a) and mezzanine (b).

with an in-suite bathroom. She also purchased a small balcony for her floor, which she placed off her bedroom overlooking the backyard.

On the third floor, Susan, along with the designer, placed the kitchen in the bay that she had selected from the menu of exterior offerings. She chose a large-size kitchen with a bar-style seating arrangement. The stacked washer and dryer were placed among the kitchen cabinets. The front end of the unit—the public zone—also contains a living and dining area. The windows on that floor were selected to accommodate these functions and to let in maximum sunlight. The private functions are located in the rear of the unit. Lisa's and Eric's bedrooms have direct access to a back balcony, the "upper backyard," that was also

Living area

Combined dining and kitchen area

Lisa's bedroom

Eric's bedroom

Views of the interior of Susan, Lisa and Eric's place.

purchased from the exterior menu. When Susan contemplated the layout of the third floor, she realized that in a few years, when the kids left home, she could combine their bedroom areas and turn them into a living room. She therefore asked the builder to install a demountable partition between the two bedrooms, which could be easily dismantled when the time came. The partition is made of gypsum boards affixed to a lightweight metal-stud core and is stuffed with insulation in order to increase its acoustic performance.

When selecting finishings for the home, Susan and the kids chose a continuous linoleum sheet for the living/dining area, hallway, and kitchen. For the rear bedrooms as well as the mezzanine, hardwood flooring was chosen.

Mezzanine lounge

Mezzanine study

Upper bedroom

Upper in-suite bathroom

Views of the interior of Susan, Lisa and Eric's place.

HOME IN A BOX

Industrial production of housing and adaptability are compatible concepts. Building a home in a plant using a systematic process holds potential for a better fit between clients and their chosen homes. Despite the sophisticated tools used in today's prefabrication, the practice itself is not new. Some even link it to the ancient Romans, who carried building parts with them on their voyages for on-site assembly. During the nineteenth century, the British advanced methods of prefabrication in order to house people on their overseas missions. One notable structure was the Portable Colonial Cottage for emigrants, a lightweight, easily erected, standardized structure made of panels and bolted together on site in less than a day. As a result of its standardized plan and repetition of elements, its production on an assembly line was facilitated (Herbert 1984).

A milestone in the development of the industrial production of housing in the modern era, and one that is significant to the work presented in this section, is the Sears, Roebuck and Company mail-order homes (Cooke and Friedman 2001). The idea of selling houses through mail-order catalogs is strange to many people today, yet it was an efficient means of conducting business that made a great deal of sense to Sears. Currently a regular department store in most major North American centers, Sears sold most types of merchandise required for the homes via mail-order catalog at the turn of the twentieth century. At this time comparatively few North Americans were living in cities, so Sears developed its infrastructure to serve its mainly rural clientele, providing everything from clothing to housing. At a time when information traveled slowly, Sears was able to reach a wide market through its catalogs. People could find out about Sears merchandise and make selections hundreds of miles from the company's head office in Chicago. For Sears, adding the sale of houses to the business was logical once technology had reached the point where prefabrication and distribution on a large scale were possible. The railroad network linked hundreds of cities and towns in the Northeast and the Midwest, and the emphasis on things modern and progressive in early-twentieth-century society created an ideal climate for the acceptance of the new building technology.

Sears had an additional reason to be interested in the housing industry. The end of the Industrial Revolution in the United States, a 50 percent increase in the country's population between 1890 and 1910, and the end of World War I in

1918 had created a significant housing crisis (Schweitzer and Davis 1990). The need for reasonably priced, well-constructed housing that could be erected quickly was acute. Seeing the opportunity for achieving a high volume of sales, Sears produced its first *Book of Modern Homes and Building Plans* in 1908. The catalog featured 22 designs priced between $650 and $2500 (Wissinger 1987).

For most home buyers, the ability to obtain machined precut and notched lumber was a remarkable advantage at a time when power tools were rare and local sawmill prices could be exorbitant. Sears's two principal lines of houses, the Standard Bilt and better-quality Honor Bilt, were precut in the factory and sent to the site in individual pieces. This meant that the majority of Sears houses were sold precut rather than fully panelized as is generally the case today. In fact, the only panelized houses sold were Simplex Cottages designed for summer use. In all cases, however, the package was complete down to the nails. All holes were bored and millwork provided, although the carpenter on site was still expected to trim the diagonally set subflooring and trim and miter external sheathing. Building paper, paint and varnishes, lumber, lath, shingles, roofing, and windows were all included (Gowans 1986). By all accounts, the materials were of excellent quality, and illustrations from Sears catalogs show that the construction techniques specified, including 14⅜-inch (375-millimeter) stud spacing, were very sound. All material sent with the order was numbered and keyed to specific blueprints of each part of the house, windows and doors were preassembled, and trim was precut and shaped. A 77-page construction manual, *How to Build Your Ready Cut Honor Bilt Home,* was included to assist customers (*Business Week* 1930).

More than a historical example, the Sears experience could have been a paradigm for the establishment of a vibrant prefabricated industry in North America. The opportunity came in the post-World War II era, when demand for lower-cost, efficiently built homes was measured in the millions. The home building industry, however, decided to pursue a more traditional route. Advances were made in the process as well as in the product. Builders perfected the method of managing the building of a house by breaking the process into a highly controlled, efficient and segregated sequence of tasks. Rather than creating an assembly line production with stationary workers and moving products, the product became stationary and trades became mobile. This process was aided by a building products industry that produced prefabricated components that fit a modular system of measurements. Batt insulation, for example, was

Advertisement showing the time saved by building a Sears Home: comparison of two houses of the same design constructed side by side, one using conventional materials and the other employing precut lumber and components.

designed to fit in the spaces between studs. Stud heights matched the length of gypsum wallboards that were affixed to them to form the room enclosures.

Millions of homes were produced over the decades in North America using conventional construction methods. Prefabrication, on the other hand, had a poor general image that did not help it gain widespread popularity with builders and the public. Unlike consumers in countries such as Sweden and Japan, where industrialized production is highly appreciated, North American buyers regard prefabricated homes as of inferior quality. Poor design and the tendency to associate prefabrication with mobile homes did not help change this perception. Another key disincentive for prefabrication was the inability of the industry to demonstrate a significant monetary advantage to a seemingly repetitive method of manufacturing.

Things have changed in recent years. Automation is now a large part of industrialized production, and computers assist in all phases of design, production, and shipping to aid in accommodating individual clients' needs. Year-round production unencumbered by poor weather conditions is another reason builders have begun to consider prefabrication. Traditionally, developers in the northern part of the continent have had to exclude winter months from their production schedules. Prefabrication has remedied that by enabling them to assemble and enclose a structure in a single day. Another reason for the inclination on the part of builders to use prefabricated homes has to do with the pull side of the market. The range of household compositions, combined with diverse lifestyles, has led builders to be more innovative in their product offerings. Industrial production methods can be a valuable tool in accommodating such diversity.

Another sign that suggests that the tide against prefabrication is turning is the boom-and-bust years that have influenced the operation of the industry. When market demand exceeds supply, builders often resort to prefabrication. Panelized production methods, for example, have made significant inroads into mainstream tract housing development. In addition, research and development on the part of manufacturers have brought to the market new products such as stressed-skin panels and have ameliorated quality in general.

The project presented here was designed to be part of this new model of the home delivery system, with the goal of better responding to the specific needs of buyers and providing them with greater choice and adaptability. The following section describes an actual process of designing an adaptable structure for prefabrication and taking part in setting up a plant in which homes are manufactured.

Mass Customization

The Home in a Box project began when the owner of a midsize Montreal building company that constructed homes conventionally decided to explore the merits of prefabrication. The advantage of reducing on-site work and adapting his products to home buyers' needs appealed to him. He was also tempted by the idea of setting up a manufacturing plant. Over the years, his home building firm constructed hundreds of units, among them the Grow Home and the Next Home, affordable and adaptable housing prototypes that were designed

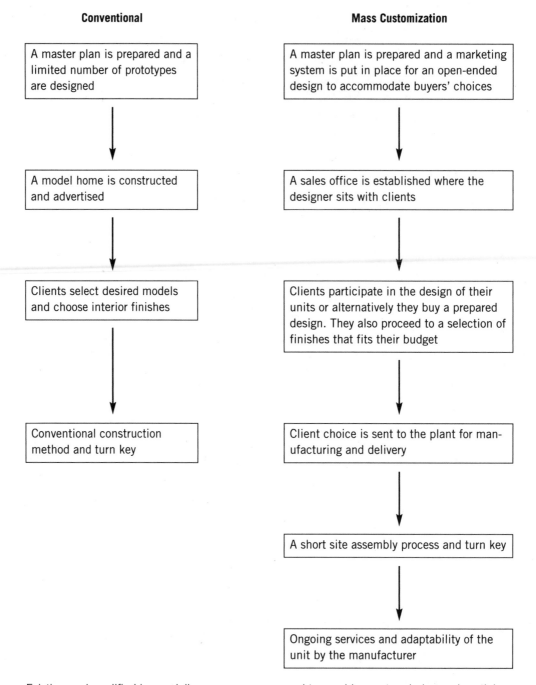

Conventional

A master plan is prepared and a limited number of prototypes are designed

A model home is constructed and advertised

Clients select desired models and choose interior finishes

Conventional construction method and turn key

Mass Customization

A master plan is prepared and a marketing system is put in place for an open-ended design to accommodate buyers' choices

A sales office is established where the designer sits with clients

Clients participate in the design of their units or alternatively they buy a prepared design. They also proceed to a selection of finishes that fits their budget

Client choice is sent to the plant for manufacturing and delivery

A short site assembly process and turn key

Ongoing services and adaptability of the unit by the manufacturer

Existing and modified home delivery process prepared to provide greater choice and participation by home buyers.

by the author and are described earlier. Through his plant, the developer wanted to offer these designs to his clients as well as to market them across North America.

In consultation with the author, the developer wanted to explore the option of mass customization of his products. His wish, which sounds like a contradiction, had been explored earlier by manufacturers of other consumer products (Anderson 1997). The concept maintains that it is possible to accommodate the unique needs of a particular customer within the existing mass manufacturing and marketing framework. In order to achieve this objective, the builder realized he would need to modify his housing delivery process. The chain of events from project initiation to turning over the keys to his customers would have to be altered.

In addition to offering predesigned models, the new process would include the opportunity to consult with a designer and have a greater preoccupancy say in fitting the interior layout to space needs and budget. Designs made according to home buyers' wishes would be transmitted from the sales office to the plant, where they would be manufactured and sent to the site for assembly. The marketing process, it was envisioned, could work from anywhere in North America. Thus, rather than creating a limited number of models, an open-ended approach would be put in place. The design was made flexible to fit the needs of a variety of markets and sites.

The next steps for the builder were to set up a manufacturing plant and to modify the design of the Grow Home and Next Home for industrial production. The author was entrusted to do the design modification. After a study that included meetings with conventional builders as well as researching a range of prefabrication methods, it was decided that panelized production would be the most suitable approach for both the plant and the designs.

Adapting Designs

The adaptation of the Grow Home and the Next Home to a manufacturing process began by creating a large number of design variations. They were based on the original concepts and their range was further narrowed according to the anticipated clients at the projects' sites. The next stage was to identify interior walls of similar length in all the design variations in both the Grow Home and

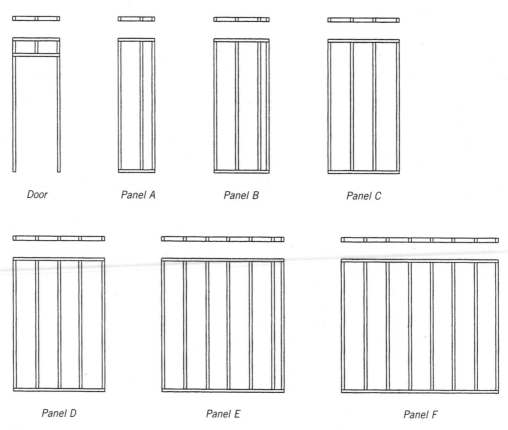

Door	Panel A	Panel B	Panel C

Panel D	Panel E	Panel F

Panel types chosen for the Grow Home and Next Home interior partitions.

Next Home. Six typical walls were found. They formed the core group of interior partition building blocks, which would be repeated in all the designs. A similar process was carried out for the exterior walls. A variety of elevations were studied to create a limited number of panels with different openings. Since the widths of the Grow Home and the Next Home were different, there were typically more exterior panels than interior partitions.

When the type and number of exterior and interior panels were determined, design simulations began. Using the typical panels, several layouts were prepared for prospective buyers. The plans would be offered as part of a prepared package for home buyers who did not wish to participate in a process of customizing the interior to their needs and budgets. Those who wished to have their needs accommodated with the help of a designer would be able to do so,

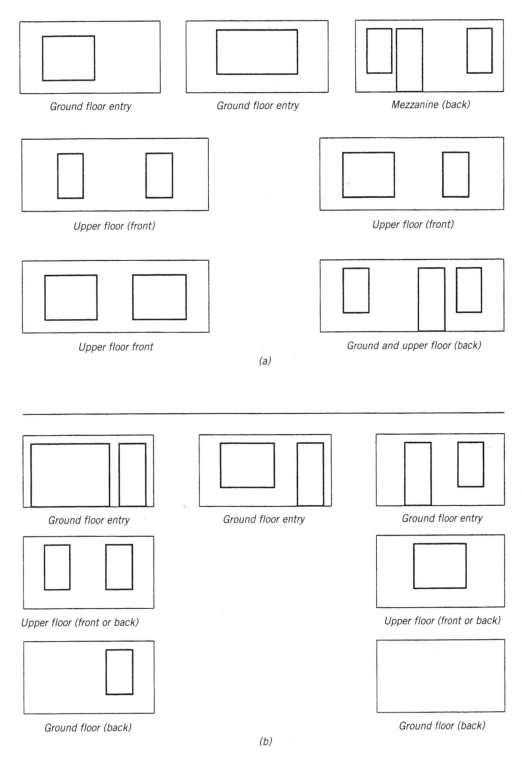

Panel types chosen for the Grow Home (a) and Next Home (b) exterior partitions.

| Ground floor | Second floor | Third floor | Mezzanine |

| Ground floor | Second floor | Third floor |

Interior layout variations for a Next Home structure arranged as a triplex: design with mezzanine (top) and without (bottom).

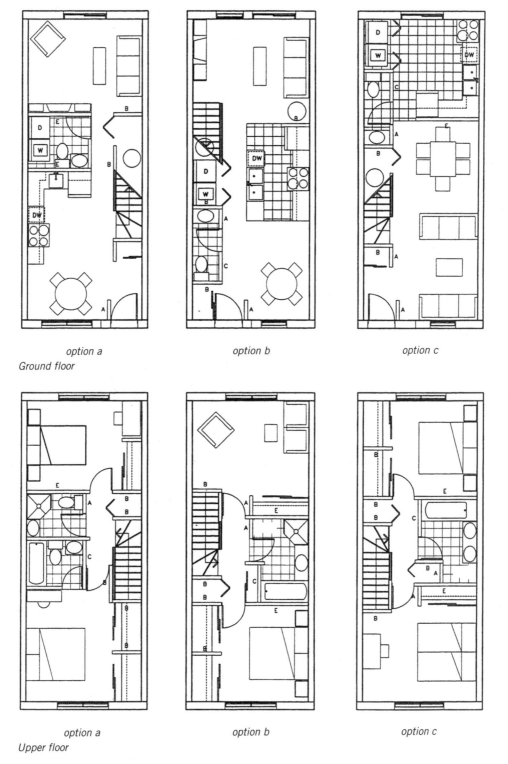

option a   option b   option c

Ground floor

option a   option b   option c

Upper floor

Interior layout variations for a Grow Home structure built in a row: three ground-floor options (top) and upper-floor options (bottom).

(a)

Panel type	Number of panels (option a)	Number of panels (option b)	Number of panels (option c)	Total
A	2	0	4	6
B	1	1	6	8
C	1	3	2	6
D	0	0	1	1
E	2	3	1	6
F	2	1	1	4
Total	8	8	15	

Next Home 20′ × 40′ with mezzanine

(b)

Panel type	Number of panels (option a)	Number of panels (option b)	Number of panels (option c)	Total
A	1	4	4	9
B	1	4	5	10
C	3	2	2	7
D	0	1	1	2
E	2	1	0	3
F	1	2	1	4
Total	8	14	13	

Next Home 20′ × 40′ without mezzanine

(c)

Panel type	Number of panels (option a)	Number of panels (option b)	Number of panels (option c)	Total
A	5	4	5	14
B	5	5	5	15
C	0	2	2	4
D	0	0	0	0
E	5	2	2	9
F	0	0	0	0
Total	15	13	14	

Grow Home

The number of panels needed for the production of a Next Home structure (a) and (b) and Grow Home (c).

using the typical exterior and interior panels in their designs. The facade design followed a similar process. A range of options was prepared, which would be offered to home buyers and perhaps even to other developers who wanted to undertake the construction of such projects. In order to facilitate the manufacturing process, tables were prepared to indicate how many panels were required for each option. When the manufacturing of a large project was undertaken, similarly sized panels could be mass produced to be used in different design layouts.

Without mezzanine

With mezzanine

Next Home

Grow Home

Facade variations using standard panels: Next Home (top) and Grow Home (bottom).

The Manufacturing Plant

The design of the manufacturing plant corresponded to the nature of the marketing process of the homes. The work stations each performed a task that, when combined, ensured rapid production. The process started in the technical office, where information was sent electronically from the sales office. Two types of designs could be received: the first was a standard prepared layout, and the second could be created in the sales office with the participation of the home buyer. A technician then calculated the type and number of panels needed. This information was sent to a cutting station where the lumber necessary for the assembly was cut to size. Then the segments were marked and delivered to semiautomated assembly stations where an on-screen display showed a worker how they should be put together. Next the interior and the exterior panels were constructed. According to the design and type of order, exterior panels would have windows installed in them. At that station, they were also insulated. The panels were then numbered and hoisted to the factory yard for storage and shipment for on-site assembly.

Designing

Cutting

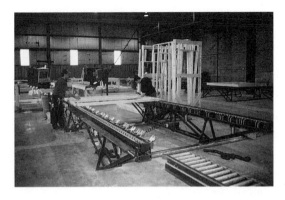

Assembly

Window and insulation installation

Shipping

Site assembly

The manufacturing process.

CHOICES IN THE FOREST

The project began when Jean-Marie Lavoie and Paul Brassard, retired architects from the Quebec City area in Quebec, Canada, purchased a 102-acre (41-hectare) plot of densely forested land. Proximity to the Saint Lawrence River with a view of the city in the far distance made the site a prime location for a housing development. The developers called the community La Forêt de Marie-Victorin after a well-known Quebec botanist.

When Lavoie and Brassard contemplated their approach to the site design and the type of homes they wished to sell, they realized that they must apply unconventional thinking to their decisions. They recognized that common approaches to contemporary development—those that involve clearing the forest and building wide boulevards—would destroy the natural beauty and uproot the trees. The homes, they also decided, should not be sprawling suburban dwellings whose construction would mean extensive alteration of the landscape. They instead agreed that adaptability to the topography needed to play a pivotal role in both urban planning and unit design. In their search for a housing prototype that would fill these requirements, they became familiar with the work of the author, with whom they collaborated in the design of both the community and the homes. The intention was to promote sustainable living and create a community that contributed to such a mind-set.

Sustainable Living

The notion of sustainable development was introduced in the mid-seventies as a result of recognition of the environmental harm that current development practices had caused. Authors and thinkers like Schumacher (1973) warned of actions that, if pursued further, could endanger the delicate balance between people and nature. Years later, this reflection led to the establishment of several international organizations that attempted to outline specific actions to remedy the situation. The World Commission on Environment and Development (WCED), also known as the Brundland Commission, is probably the best-known international initiative. In their report, *Our Common Future* (1987), the commissioners defined sustainable development as "development that meets the present without compromising the ability of future generations to meet their own needs." A conceptual approach whereby every present action has to be taken while considering its future effect on the environment was put in place.

When broken into subcomponents, three main aspects are seen as influencing the functioning of a sustainable community. The first is society itself: the people who reside in the development, their demographic makeup, and their lifestyles. The economic vitality of the development is also an essential aspect, since monetary failure will cause the enterprise to cease to exist. The final factor is the environment itself—its many facets, which include the built components and nature. Only when a balance is struck between these three elements that takes the future into consideration is sustainable development possible.

Since the turn of the twentieth century, and especially after World War II, bad development practices have begun to take their toll. There were many ramifications to such practices in which the environment was one of the main casualties. Forested landscape was cleared to make room for wide roads. Vast green spaces were covered with sod that needed large quantities of fresh water during dry summer months. The homes themselves swelled in size. North Americans consumed domestic space much like any other product. The design of homes became more intricate and complex, leading to the use of many scarce natural resources, of which lumber was the main one. Once built, the homes burdened the environment by using energy to keep them warm in winter and cool in summer, consuming fresh water and draining gray water, and creating domestic waste. Such activities had a damaging effect on both the local and global environments.

It was recognized that old practices needed to be abandoned and new ones put in place. Sustainable residential development set out to reduce reliance on cars by encouraging pedestrian activities and a mix of commercial and residential uses. Alternative building products and practices that consume fewer natural resources are becoming widespread. Attention is being paid to constructing better-insulated homes that consume less energy, and designers position the houses better to maximize passive solar gain. The proliferation of telecommunications and the popularity of working at home have also reduced travel time and enabled the mixing of commercial and domestic activities within the same residence.

These processes all demonstrate that what is needed and has perhaps begun is an adaptable mind-set, one that recognizes that present actions bear future consequences. We integrated such a mind-set in the design of La Forêt de Marie-Victorin.

Adapting to Nature

The first stage in the development of the master plan began by taking stock of the site's existing conditions. There were small- and large-scale aspects that were considered in the design. Two areas with dense concentrations of trees were documented: the first was on the northern edge of the site and the second in a ravine in the middle. Both areas run in an east-west direction. On a small scale, throughout the site there were many impressive rocky areas with large, visible boulders that created a magnificent formation worth preserving. Many trees on the site were old growth.

After the site characteristics were completed, objectives were set for the design of the roads. In order to keep nature intact, it was decided that circulation should be as short as possible. Also, unlike typical suburban streets measuring 40 feet (12.2 meters) wide, a 20-foot (6.1-meter) road was designed. The sidewalks were only 18 inches (455 millimeters) wide and were at the same level as the street's asphalt surface, letting rain water return to nature where it belonged. The street path was routed according to the site elevations, bypassing boulders and refraining from cutting trees. During the construction, all services were buried under the road, again to maintain the natural beauty of the place.

The land subdivision was another design aspect that required deviation from the common approach. Rather than lots with 60 × 100-foot (18.3 × 30.5-meter) dimensions, it was recognized that long, narrow lots would be more suitable for the site. Smaller homes in denser configurations could be assembled rather than encouraging the building of large units. While considering the design, we recognized that the practice of clearing trees from the entire lot should be discouraged by enacting a requirement in the deed of sale that only those trees that grew on the footprint of the home would be cut. The rest would be protected during construction and would remain untouched. The dense areas in the middle and at the top of the site, it was decided, would be turned into a communal park to be used by all the inhabitants.

Another important decision that helped preserve the site was to place the homes as close as possible to the road, thereby preventing cutting down of trees. Carports were offered as an option and would be placed in front of the house or next to it. In order to reduce the need for utility poles to carry tele-

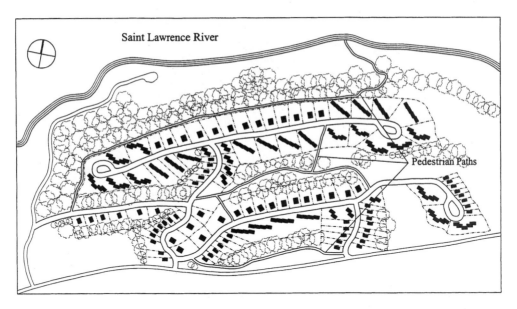

The objective of the site plan of La Forêt de Marie-Victorin was to reduce the amount of trees needed to be cleared in order to build roads and homes.

phone, electricity, and cable TV, a service column was constructed in front of each house. The column would be the exit for all the underground services that were placed under the road. It would also be the place where a domestic recycling box would be located for general collection.

Fitting Homes to the Landscape

The quest for a home with a long and narrow footprint that would prevent the clearing of many trees led to the development of a unit measuring 20 × 32 feet (6.1 × 9.8 meters). The design created floors of 640 square feet (64 square meters), each of which could become a self-contained one-bedroom apartment. Here, too, a variety of typologies was offered. Units could be built as two- or three-story structures to accommodate one or several households. When a three-story was offered, it too could be divided into one or more units. There could also be a range of internal configurations to accommodate a variety of household compositions.

(a)   (b)

The narrow roads bypass boulders and reduce the number of trees that need to be cleared (a). During construction of the shallow foundation, the trees surrounding the site were wrapped to protect them (b).

Recognizing the effect that extensive excavation and dynamiting would have on the environment, the construction of a basement level was avoided. A shallow foundation was constructed instead, and the attic of the structure was taken advantage of. A special truss design was selected that allowed the maximum use of this area. Turning the attic into a habitable space also aided in resource conservation. Since warm air rises, there would be a reduced need to heat the space during the winter months. Special precautions were taken during construction to protect the trees, which were wrapped to guard against damage caused by heavy machinery.

Keeping the Options Open

In order to maximize choice and adaptability in the unit design, an appropriate floor plan had to be created. Locating all the unit's wet functions and services along one of the walls proved to be a suitable strategy, as it freed the rest of the space for interior partitioning that fit the occupants' needs and budgets. As a result, the stairs, kitchen, bathrooms, and utilities were all placed against the north wall. This strategy had another advantage: preventing the fenestration of that wall led to a reduction in energy losses. It also contributed to increasing

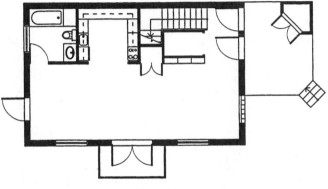

Ground floor

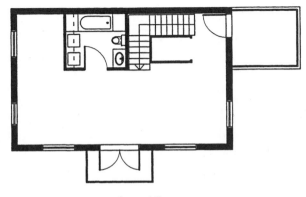

Second floor

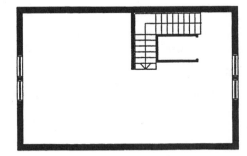

Attic

The stairs, wet functions, and utilities were placed against the northern wall, freeing the rest of the space for buyers' choice and reducing energy losses.

Most openings were placed in the southern facade (middle) to maximize passive solar gain.

privacy with regard to the neighboring home. The openings were placed instead on the other facades and mostly on the southern elevation to increase exposure and maximize passive solar gain.

The open-ended approach to the design provided an opportunity to create a variety of interior configurations. The next step was to develop a range of options for each floor. The options created a possible scenario whereby the ground floor could be used as an independent dwelling unit to house an elderly member of the family. Alternatively, the floor could become a home office for a household that would reside on the upper two floors. It was expected that, as with a menu, buyers would select their needed number of floors, desired interior layout, and suitable finishes.

In order to maximize the flexibility of the overall space arrangement, two front doors were designed. This provided the opportunity to make the structure into a single- or multifamily home. Also, the configuration of the stairs would permit simple installation of an internal elevator to let a disabled person reach all the levels.

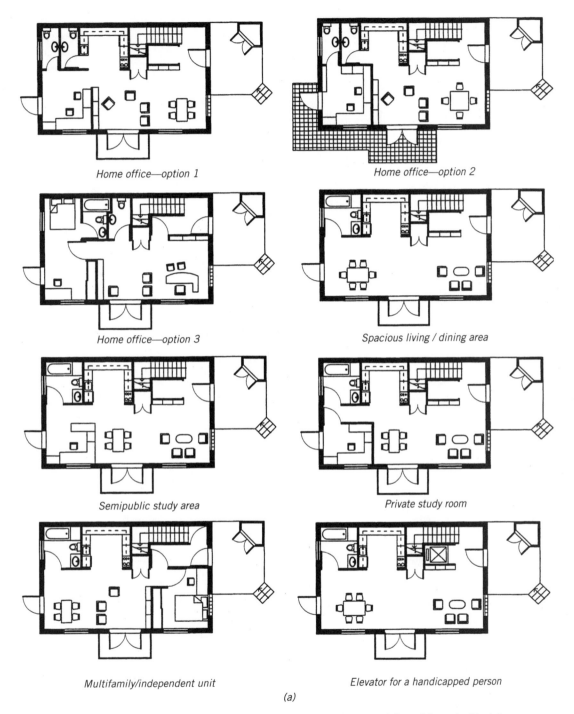

Home office—option 1

Home office—option 2

Home office—option 3

Spacious living / dining area

Semipublic study area

Private study room

Multifamily/independent unit

Elevator for a handicapped person

(a)

Floor plans showing design alternatives for the ground floor (a), second floor (b), and attic (c).

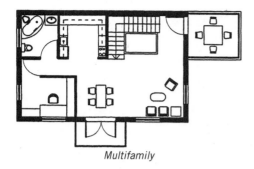

Multifamily

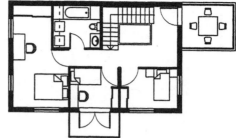

Three-bedroom arrangement

Master bedroom

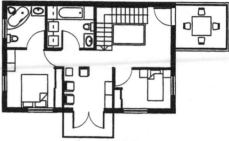

Second living area

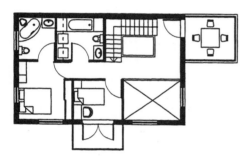

Atrium open to ground floor

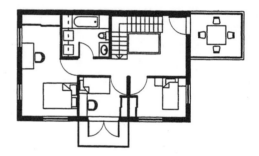

Private study room

(b)

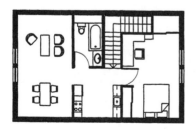

Multifamily/independent unit

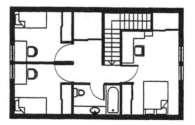

Three-bedroom arrangement

(c)

(Continued)

Ground floor: *The living/dining area*

The bathroom

Second floor: *Family space*

The child's bedroom

Attic: *Master bedroom*

The home office in the rear

The model unit was partitioned and decorated to house a dual-headed family with a child, where one of the parents has a home office.

ADAPTING FOR SPECIAL NEEDS

When homes are designed, unless they are initially fitted for use by elderly or disabled people, their designers envision able clients using them. The notion that years later the occupants may become frail, confined to a wheelchair, or unable to use simple fixtures like the faucets seems remote. The project presented here was designed to accommodate the needs of occupants who were diagnosed and notified about a debilitating illness prior to the purchase of their homes. During occupancy they experienced deteriorating health conditions that required ongoing fitting of their units. Measures taken during design and construction facilitated adaptation of the homes to the residents' needs.

The design was an entry by a team led by the author to a Canada Mortgages and Housing Corporation (CMHC) Flex Housing national competition in which the project was recognized. The team attempted to put forward the view that occupants who were either disabled or elderly were better served by being enabled to remain in their own homes, where they could enjoy independent living.

Enabling the elderly to age in place or the disabled to function in their own residences is regarded as contributing to the occupants' health and self-esteem. In addition, the notion of installing in the unit devices on which the resident will be highly dependent is seen as a wrong strategy. Rather, these devices need only to fill the gap between a domestic task—using the shower, for example—and a limiting physical condition. This general mind-set is also a result of recognition by governments that as the number of elderly people is expected to rise with the retirement of the Baby Boom generation, institutional care will not be available to, or affordable by, all. Rather, encouraging people to better use their homes by fitting them out is the preferred approach. This mind-set is also largely supported by legislation in many countries that has mandated accommodating disabled people in their homes and in public places. In the United States, under the access requirement for housing programs receiving federal financial assistance covered by Section 504 of the Rehabilitation Act of 1973, 5 percent of new apartments had to be wheelchair accessible. The Fair Housing Act Amendment (FHAA) of 1988 established a special and different accessibility standard for rental of multifamily housing. The Act mandated a lower level of accessibility but

(a)

(b)

(c)

Front (a), side (b), and rear (c) elevations of the Next Home demonstration unit.

Fabrication of panels

Constructing the foundation and first floor

First-floor panel

Prefabricated roof trusses

Applying stucco to the exterior

Installing plumbing fixtures

Wiring the structure

Drywall and plaster

Tiling the bathrooms

Painting

Installing floating floors

Assembling kitchen cabinets

Construction process of the Next Home.

The front home office

The kitchen/dining area

The living space with exit to back patio

The bedroom space

Views of the ground-floor unit's interior.

Kitchen

Living and dining area

Bedroom

Multipurpose room

Views of the second floor unit's interior.

Living area

Combined dining and kitchen area

Lisa's bedroom

Eric's bedroom

Mezzanine lounge

Mezzanine study

Upper bedroom

Upper in-suite bathroom

Views of the interior of Susan, Lisa and Eric's place.

(a)

(b)

The narrow roads bypass boulders and reduce the number of trees that need to be cleared (a). During construction of the shallow foundation, the trees surrounding the site were wrapped to protect them (b).

Most openings were placed in the southern facade (top) to maximize passive solar gain.

Ground floor: *The living/dining area*

The bathroom

Second floor: *Family space*

The child's bedroom

Attic: *Master bedroom*

The home office in the rear

The model unit was partitioned and decorated to house a dual-headed family with a child, where one of the parents has a home office.

covered a greater number of apartments. The Americans with Disabilities Act of 1990 (ADA) looked at institutional and public facilities. In hotels, for example, the standard required that a limited number of units be accessible. The legislation is an indication that the public and the building industry at large are starting to take a more inclusive approach to the needs of the disabled.

Fitting a home for use by the occupants at the later stages of their lives or by special groups might have a limited advantage as opposed to making it usable throughout the whole residency. Universal design promotes the need to design housing—or any building, for that matter—to be usable by everybody at all times. An example of this approach is raising the height of electrical receptacles from their current low position so that plugging in appliances becomes simple for all. Despite the fact that special assistance is offered in the projects described here, the general approach of universal design—that of incorporating consumer products and design features that are easily usable and commonly available—was adopted.

The Context

The houses described in the following scenario were constructed as part of a large tract housing development. The units are semidetached, two-story homes with no basements and were built at a density of 15 units per acre (37 units per hectare). The marketing strategy adopted by the development firm was to offer buyers the opportunity to purchase the number of levels that they wanted and to assist them in arranging the interior according to their budget and liking. Thus, the units could be constructed as side-by-side double or single-family units.

What set this project apart from other developments was the realization that according to marketing studies large numbers of elderly people who wished to sell single-family houses were expected to look for new houses in the area. This group of buyers would need smaller units that they could fit out specially in order to enable them to age in place. The developers therefore engaged an expert to consult with the project's designers about issues related to adaptability for people with disabilities or limited mobility. A menu was created that featured special arrangements and products related to specific needs of the anticipated home buyers—for example, kitchen and bathroom configurations for occupants who use a wheelchair.

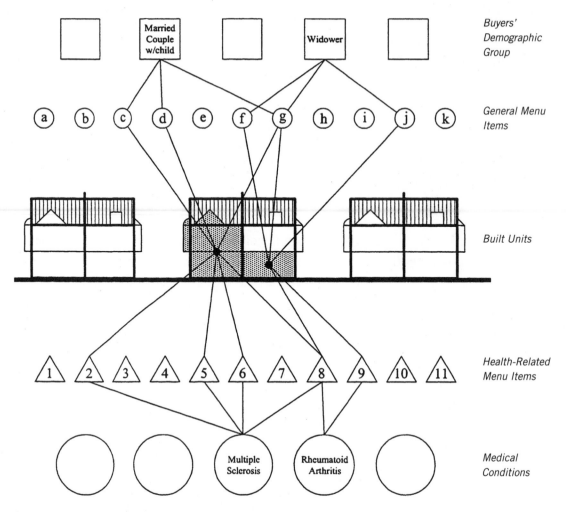

A chart describing the marketing method and the offering of components to anticipated home buyers.

On the other end of the scale, due to the unit's affordable cost, the site was also expected to attract young first-time home buyers. Those buyers would have diverse lifestyles, which required the builder to be more flexible in the interior choices and layout. As a result, a general menu of interior and exterior features was also created and displayed to home buyers in the sales office.

In order to illustrate the design process, the strategies, and the components used in adapting dwellings for occupants with special needs, two units have

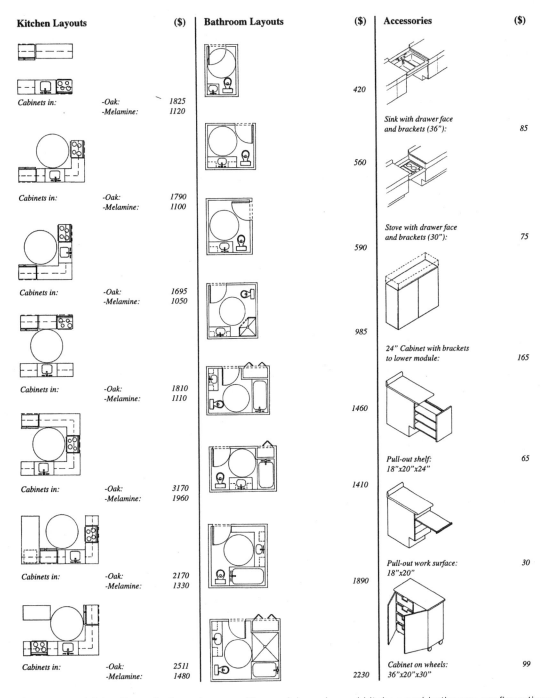

Kitchen Layouts		($)	Bathroom Layouts	($)	Accessories	($)

Kitchen Layouts:

Cabinets in: -Oak: 1825 / -Melamine: 1120

Cabinets in: -Oak: 1790 / -Melamine: 1100

Cabinets in: -Oak: 1695 / -Melamine: 1050

Cabinets in: -Oak: 1810 / -Melamine: 1110

Cabinets in: -Oak: 3170 / -Melamine: 1960

Cabinets in: -Oak: 2170 / -Melamine: 1330

Cabinets in: -Oak: 2511 / -Melamine: 1480

Bathroom Layouts:

420

560

590

985

1460

1410

1890

2230

Accessories:

Sink with drawer face and brackets (36"): 85

Stove with drawer face and brackets (30"): 75

24" Cabinet with brackets to lower module: 165

Pull-out shelf: 18"x20"x24" — 65

Pull-out work surface: 18"x20" — 30

Cabinet on wheels: 36"x20"x30" — 99

A menu containing items for homebuyers with special needs, and kitchen and bathroom configurations for occupants using a wheelchair. (All prices are in Canadian dollars.)

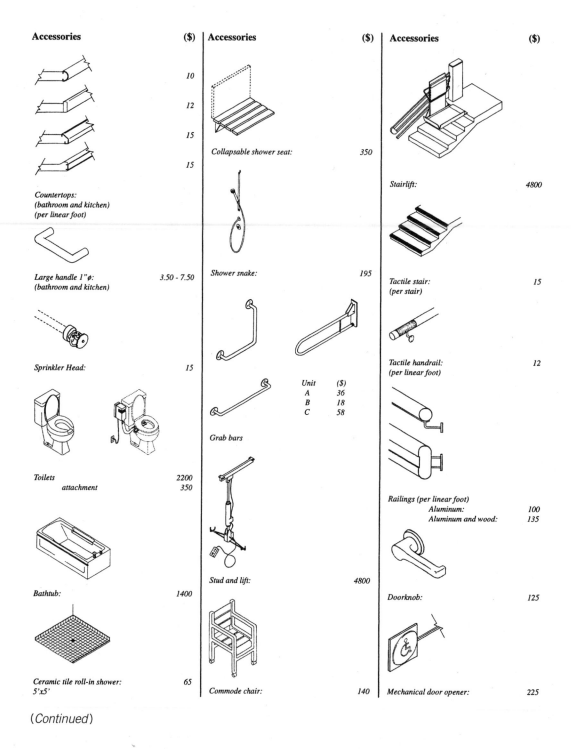

Accessories	($)	Accessories	($)	Accessories	($)

Accessories ($)

10

12

15

15

Countertops:
(bathroom and kitchen)
(per linear foot)

Large handle 1"ø: 3.50 - 7.50
(bathroom and kitchen)

Sprinkler Head: 15

Toilets 2200
    attachment 350

Bathtub: 1400

Ceramic tile roll-in shower: 65
5'x5'

Accessories ($)

Collapsable shower seat: 350

Shower snake: 195

Unit	($)
A	36
B	18
C	58

Grab bars

Stud and lift: 4800

Commode chair: 140

Accessories ($)

Stairlift: 4800

Tactile stair: 15
(per stair)

Tactile handrail: 12
(per linear foot)

Railings (per linear foot)
    Aluminum: 100
    Aluminum and wood: 135

Doorknob: 125

Mechanical door opener: 225

(Continued)

been chosen. The first was purchased by a young couple with a 3-year-old daughter. Shortly prior to buying the unit, Ann, the mother, was diagnosed with multiple sclerosis (MS). Her situation was expected to deteriorate—for which the unit was to be prepared. The couple had purchased both stories of a semi-detached two-story structure. Richard, a 60-year-old widower, purchased the lower unit in the adjacent structure. For a year prior to buying his house, Richard had been experiencing symptoms of rheumatoid arthritis (RA), with which he was diagnosed. The unit was therefore prepared for gradual deterioration caused by that illness.

The buyers of this project were given an opportunity to coordinate between exterior openings and interior functions as well as to personalize their facades. The choices made by the occupants are presented in the following sections.

Front elevation

Rear elevation

Side elevation

Side elevation

Facades of the semidetached building. Ann and her family occupy two stories of the left structure, and Richard occupies the bottom story of the right structure.

Ann's Place

Ann's illness, MS, is a progressive disease of the central nervous system in which the protective covering of nerve fibers in the brain and spinal cord is destroyed. It is characterized by episodes of remission and exacerbation. Symptoms range from numbness and tingling to paralysis and incontinence, and changes in cognition and judgment are also frequently seen. There is no cure for MS; however, studies have shown that with intensive rehabilitative therapy, there is a decrease in the number of limitations experienced by patients in areas such as self-care, bed and wheelchair mobility, bladder control, and household tasks. This means that patients can manage on their own at home instead of in a hospital or other institution, which is beneficial not only in terms of health care costs, but, more importantly, in terms of the patient's independence and dignity.

Shortly before purchasing her home, Ann noticed numbness and a sensation of pins and needles in her fingers throughout the day. She visited her family physician, who referred her to a neurologist. After a series of tests, the neurologist informed her that she was suffering from MS. She was told that her symptoms might disappear completely but then return within two years, only more severely and with additional symptoms.

In consultation with her physician, Ann realized she had to prepare herself to cope with an illness whose deteriorating condition would severely curtail her functioning at home. As a result, she decided to purchase a unit and prepare it for the installation of components that would allow her to continue to function independently at home. She and her family therefore purchased and specially fit a two-story unit of a semidetached structure.

Two years after occupancy, Ann began to notice a decrease in her vision: objects appeared blurry and her field of vision was darker. A few days later, the awkward sensation and numbness returned to her hands and was also present in her feet. At times, Ann felt like she might lose her balance, and she developed a fear of falling. Her family was concerned about her safety at home, especially since she had tripped and fallen on several occasions. She was hospitalized for five days, and when she returned home she was visited by an occupational therapist and a physical therapist.

The physical therapist provided Ann with a series of exercises to maintain her strength so that she could remain as independent as possible. The occupa-

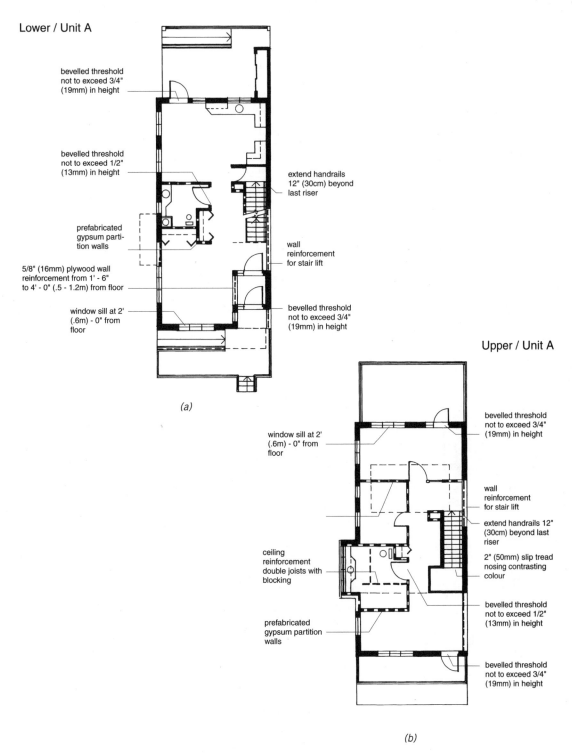

Lower / Unit A

bevelled threshold
not to exceed 3/4"
(19mm) in height

bevelled threshold
not to exceed 1/2"
(13mm) in height

prefabricated
gypsum partition walls

5/8" (16mm) plywood wall
reinforcement from 1' - 6"
to 4' - 0" (.5 - 1.2m) from floor

window sill at 2'
(.6m) - 0" from
floor

extend handrails
12" (30cm) beyond
last riser

wall
reinforcement
for stair lift

bevelled threshold
not to exceed 3/4"
(19mm) in height

(a)

Upper / Unit A

window sill at 2'
(.6m) - 0" from
floor

ceiling
reinforcement
double joists with
blocking

prefabricated
gypsum partition
walls

bevelled threshold
not to exceed 3/4"
(19mm) in height

wall
reinforcement
for stair lift

extend handrails 12"
(30cm) beyond last
riser

2" (50mm) slip tread
nosing contrasting
colour

bevelled threshold
not to exceed 1/2"
(13mm) in height

bevelled threshold
not to exceed 3/4"
(19mm) in height

(b)

Lower floor (a) and upper floor (b) plans that were purchased by Ann and her family and fitted upon construction for coping with the gradual deterioration associated with Ann's multiple sclerosis.

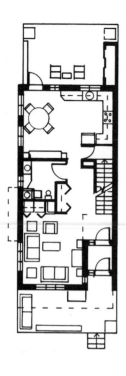

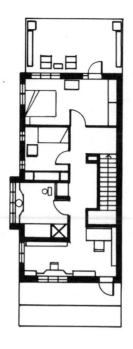

Occupancy

The home was prepared for future adaptation and the addition of components. Corridor width as well as door-step and window height are all adjusted.

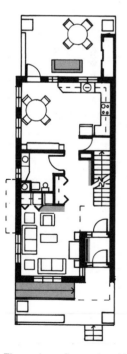

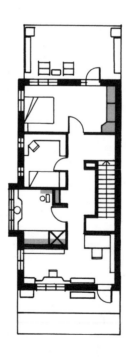

Two Years After Occupancy

Exacerbation of symptoms. A ramp is installed in the front. Grab bars are installed near the toilet and the bathtub. Cupboard shelves are adjusted in the master bedroom.

Floor plans (lower level left, upper level right) showing the progressive adaptation of Ann's two-story home to the conditions of her illness. The shaded area indicates items that have been added in order to assist Ann in carrying out specific tasks.

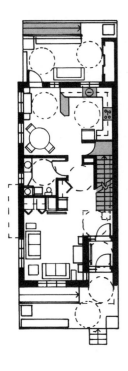
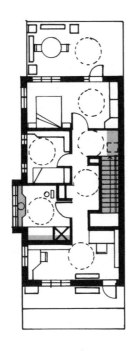

Four Years After Occupancy

Wheelchair-bound. A ramp is installed in the rear. A lift is affixed to the stairs. Sinks are adjusted and a counter constructed in the kitchen. Automatic shut-offs are installed on all appliances.

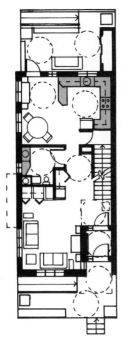
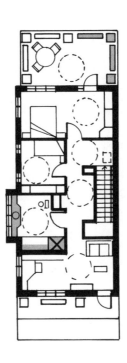

Ten Years After Occupancy

Kitchen and bathroom cabinets are all adjusted. A hand-held shower and a commode are installed in the upper bathroom.

(*Continued*)

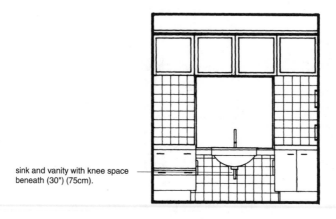

sink and vanity with knee space
beneath (30") (75cm).

Bathroom Elevation-Unit A

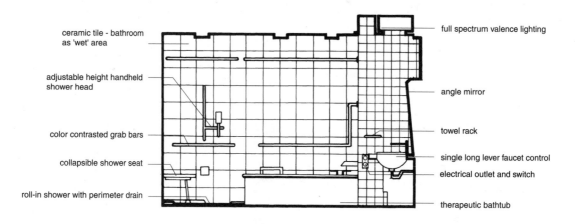

ceramic tile - bathroom
as 'wet' area

adjustable height handheld
shower head

color contrasted grab bars

collapsible shower seat

roll-in shower with perimeter drain

full spectrum valence lighting

angle mirror

towel rack

single long lever faucet control

electrical outlet and switch

therapeutic bathtub

Bathroom Elevation-Unit A

(a)

Section and elevation of specially fitted rooms in Ann's home: two views of the bathroom (a) and
kitchen (b).

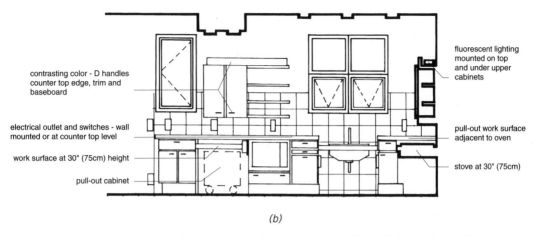

contrasting color - D handles
counter top edge, trim and
baseboard

electrical outlet and switches - wall
mounted or at counter top level

work surface at 30" (75cm) height

pull-out cabinet

fluorescent lighting
mounted on top
and under upper
cabinets

pull-out work surface
adjacent to oven

stove at 30" (75cm)

(b)

Section and elevation of specially fitted rooms in Ann's home: two views of the bathroom (a) and kitchen (b).

tional therapist evaluated her and found that she was having difficulty with hand coordination that made it difficult to perform simple cooking and self-care tasks. The therapist recommended adaptive equipment and strategic techniques to simplify tasks or make them more manageable.

The loss of balance and difficulty walking required Ann to use a cane occasionally, as well as to install a handrail in the hallway and grab bars in the bath and at the toilet. When her energy levels were low, the occupational therapist recommended that she use a bath bench in the shower to limit standing time, and he rearranged and lowered objects to mid-range level in order not to force Ann to reach too high or too low (e.g., frequently used pots were placed on top of counter to avoid bending down). As Ann's visual acuity decreased, the light switches were changed from white to black, and the counter, drawers, and stairs were outlined with a contrasting color in order to make them more noticeable.

Four years after occupancy, Ann's health deteriorated further. She was hospitalized for a short period and then returned home. Severe weakness and inability to walk forced her to become wheelchair-bound. More changes were introduced to the home. A lift to help Ann reach the upper floors was installed, and early preparation for installation of an outdoor ramp simplified entry into the house. Initial designs that considered width of doors and access ways facilitated the use of the wheelchair. In order to further conserve Ann's energy while using the kitchen, all the cupboard contents were rearranged, a central vacuum was installed, and all the doorknobs were replaced with easy-to-operate handles.

Ten years after occupancy, Ann experienced an additional decline in her physical abilities, problem-solving skills, and memory functions. She required more assistance with washing and bathing and small domestic tasks. A shower with a commode chair was installed to let her bathe independently. Water temperature had to be monitored, however, since Ann had decreased sensation in her hands.

Richard's Place

Richard, the occupant of the lower floor in the unit adjacent to Ann's, was diagnosed with RA, an autoimmune disease in which the immune system attacks the body's own tissues. It is characterized by periods of exacerbation and remission, which vary in severity. Joint inflammation is the most common clinical manifestation. The joints become swollen, red, warm, painful, and stiff. Internal structures around the joints become weak, resulting in slow deterioration, weakness, and eventual deformity. The finger joints are most commonly affected, resulting in a weak grip. RA may also involve other areas such as the hips, knees, ankles, or feet. Early morning stiffness is common, and sufferers may require help getting out of bed and dressing. As with other degenerative diseases, the objective of treatment is to maintain patients' physical, psychological, and functional abilities so that they can live as independently as possible.

Prior to purchasing his unit, Richard began to experience symptoms of RA. His hands were stiff and slightly painful in the mornings, and he found himself dropping articles such as his toothbrush simply because he had suddenly lost the strength to hold them. In consultation with a physician and later a therapist, Richard was told that he should prepare himself for the deteriorating conditions of RA. He and his wife decided to sell their large home and purchase a unit fitted for the installation of components that would help him age in his home with independence.

A year after moving into his unit, Richard experienced a decrease in energy level and began to adjust his activities. He was able to sit in his bath, but he

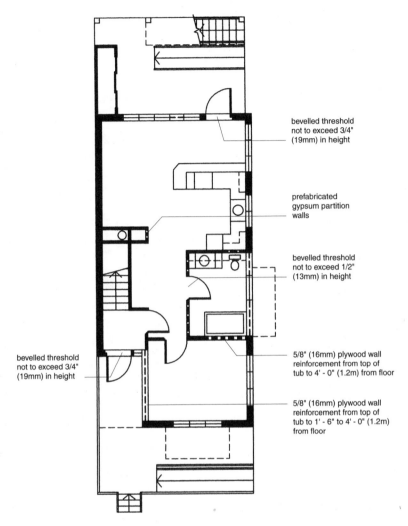

bevelled threshold
not to exceed 3/4"
(19mm) in height

prefabricated
gypsum partition
walls

bevelled threshold
not to exceed 1/2"
(13mm) in height

bevelled threshold
not to exceed 3/4"
(19mm) in height

5/8" (16mm) plywood wall
reinforcement from top of
tub to 4' - 0" (1.2m) from floor

5/8" (16mm) plywood wall
reinforcement from top of
tub to 1' - 6" to 4' - 0" (1.2m)
from floor

Floor plan of Richard's home which upon construction was prepared for installation of components to help him cope independently with rheumatoid arthritis.

required a transfer board to get in and he used a hand-held shower to avoid bending. He benefited from adjustments that were made to the unit early on, including raising the electrical outlets to prevent bending.

Eight years after occupancy, the RA affected Richard's right knee and hip as well as his hands. He used a cane, since walking was painful, and required a handrail in the hallway and the kitchen. Grab bars and a nonslip surface were

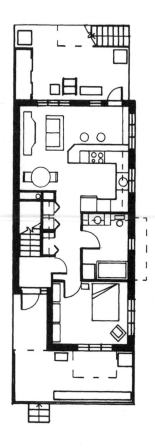

Occupancy

The unit was prepared for the progressive introduction of components relevant to Richard's illness as well as for use by a wheelchair-bound person.

Eight Years After Occupancy

Handrails are installed in the hallway and kitchen. Grab bars are installed near the toilet and bathtub.

Floor plans showing the adaptation of Richard's single-story unit to the progressive condition of his illness. The shaded areas indicate the added items.

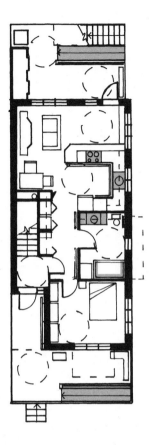

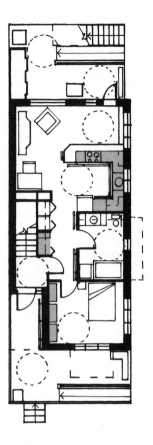

Thirteen Years After Occupancy

A wheelchair transfer board and hand-held shower are installed in the bath. Outdoor ramps are installed in the front and rear.

Eighteen Years After Occupancy

Cupboards in the kitchen and bathroom are adjusted. Hanger heights are also adjusted in the closet.

Down light - center over number and lock

Surface mounted number (10") (25cm) color contrast

Surface mounted mailbox with flat lockable top (shelf)

Handrails extend 12" (30cm)

Color side panel to contrast with door

Lever handle with lock above

Intercom and automatic door opener

Waterproof electrical outlet

Kickplate

Entry Door Elevation

(a)

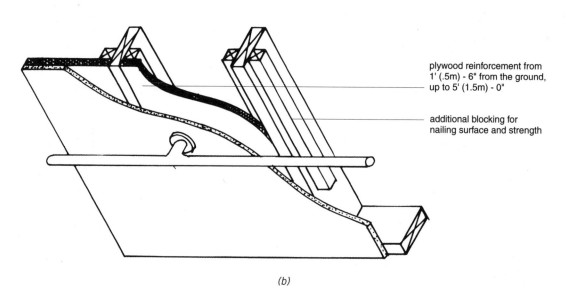

plywood reinforcement from 1' (.5m) - 6" from the ground, up to 5' (1.5m) - 0"

additional blocking for nailing surface and strength

(b)

Details of special fittings and adjustments made to Richard's unit's exterior (a) and interior wall reinforcement (b).

installed in the bath and by the toilet for physical support. Window boxes for gardening were positioned at mid-range to avoid unnecessary bending and reaching.

Approximately 13 years after his occupancy, Richard fell and fractured his right hip, which necessitated a partial hip replacement. The height of his bed was adjusted for transferring, and wheelchair ramps were installed at the front and rear entrances. The width of the doorways and corridors, which were originally designed for wheelchair use, assisted Richard's mobility. The shelves in the kitchen and bathroom cupboards, however, needed to be adjusted to enable Richard to access them from his wheelchair seat. Doorknobs were replaced with handles to make grasping easier and to require less strength to operate.

Eighteen years after occupancy, as Richard approached his eighties, he experienced a steady decline with very painful mornings. He occasionally required assistance for dressing and eating, and for transfer from wheelchair to toilet and bed. Cupboard drawers in the kitchen and bathroom were at the appropriate height, as well as drawers and hangers in the bedroom so that Richard could choose his own clothes. He needed assistance with the ramps outside and was awaiting delivery of an electric wheelchair.

The forethought and preparation given to both Ann's and Richard's homes enabled them to adapt their residences to the limits imposed upon them by their illnesses so that they could live independently and care for themselves with dignity.

"The Adjustable House." *House and Home,* vol. 2, no. 6 (December), pp. 114–116, 1952.

Alnemer, A., T. Cheng, B. Sternthal, and D. Wlodarczyk-Karzynska. "The La Prairie Experiment" (design project; instructor, Avi Friedman). Montreal, PQ: McGill School of Architecture Affordable Homes Program, 1993.

Anderson, D. M. *Agile Product Development for Mass Customization.* Chicago: Irwin, 1997.

Baxter, B., R. Belanger, M. Fritschij, E. Peterson, J. Ritchie, N. Shoiry, and G. Wong. *Suburban Planning for Affordability: Saint-Bruno-de-Montarville.* Montreal, PQ: McGill School of Architecture Affordable Homes Program (summary of design project; instructors, A. Friedman and W. Rybczynski).

Buwalda, J. "EMAD Expandable Minimum Ameryah Dwelling." *Open House International,* no. 2, pp. 61–70, 1980.

Canada Mortgage and Housing Corporation (CMHC). *New Made-to-Convert Housing.* Ottawa, ON: CMHC, 1988.

———. *Habitable Attics: New Potential for an Old Idea.* Ottawa, ON: CMHC, 1991.

Cardinal and Hardy Architects. "The Next Home Concept: Proposition Site Paul-Sauvé," Montreal, Canada (project design; in collaboration with Avi Friedman). Cardinal and Hardy Architects, 1994.

Carstens, D. Y. "Housing and Outdoor Spaces for the Elderly," in *People Places: Design Guidelines for Urban Open Spaces,* C. Cooper Marcus and C. Francis, eds. New York: Van Nostrand Reinhold, 1992.

"Convertible Plan." *Architectural Forum,* vol. 90 (April), pp. 126–130, 1949.

Cooke, A. and A. Friedman. "Ahead of Their Time: The Sears Catalogue Prefabricated Houses." *Journal of Design History,* vol. 14, no. 1, pp. 53–70, 2001.

Corredor, G. *Space Syntax Analysis of Montreal Plex Transformations* (unpublished M.Arch. report). Montreal, PQ: McGill School of Architecture, 2000.

Deilmann, H., J. C. Kirschenmann, and H. Pfeiffer. *The Dwelling*. Stuttgart, Germany: Karl Kramer Verlag, 1973.

Dirisamer, R., F. Kuznich, O. Uho, W. Voss, and J. P. Weber. "Project Dwelling of Tomorrow: Hollabrunn, Austria." *Industrialization Forum,* vol. 7, no. 1, pp. 11–16, 1976.

Dluhosch, E. "Flexibility/Variability and Programming." *Industrialization Forum,* vol. 6, no. 3–4, pp. 39–46, 1974.

Eichler, N. *The Merchant Builders*. Cambridge, MA: MIT Press, 1982.

Friedman, A. *Growth and Adaptability (G&A) in Housing* (unpublished M.Arch. thesis). Montreal, PQ: McGill School of Architecture, 1982.

———. "Innovation and the North American Homebuilding Industry." *Open House International,* vol. 14, no. 3, pp. 16–19, 1989.

———. "The Evolution of Design Characteristics during the Post-Second-World-War Housing Boom: The US Experience." *Journal of Design History,* vol. 8, no. 2, pp. 131–146, 1995.

———, "Flexible Planning Strategies: The La Prairie Experiment." *Plan Canada,* vol. 36, no. 2, pp. 33–42, 1996.

———. *The Grow Home*. Montreal, PQ: McGill-Queen's University Press, 2001.

———, and M. Pantelopoulos. "Space Management in Montreal's Wartime Homes." *Housing and Society,* vol. 23, no. 2, pp. 65–83, 1996.

———, D. Morin, and F. Dufaux (project design). Design of 119-unit Community in Aylmer, Quebec, Canada 1994.

———, V. Cammalleri, J. Nicell, F. Dufaux, and J. Green. *Sustainable Residential Developments: Planning, Design and Construction Principles ("Greening the Grow Home")*. Ottawa, ON: Canada Mortgage and Housing Corporation, 1993.

———, D. Krawitz, J. Fréchette, C. Bilimoria, and D. Raphael. *The Next Home*. Montreal, PQ: McGill School of Architecture Affordable Homes Program, 1996.

———, ———, M. Senbel, D. Raphael, J. E. Steffel, J. S. Fréchette, and J. Watt. *Planning the New Suburbia: Flexibility by Design*. Vancouver, BC: UBC Press, 2001.

Goodovitch, I. M. "Apartment Adapted to the Stages of Growth of the Family," in *Israel Builds 1977,* E. Harlap (ed.). Jerusalem, Israel: Ministry of Housing, 1977.

Gowans, A. *The Comfortable House: North American Suburban Architecture, 1890–1930*. Cambridge, MA: MIT Press, 1986.

Habraken, N. J. *Supports: An Alternative to Mass Housing*. London, UK: Architectural Press, 1972.

Hamdi, N., N. Wilkinson, and J. Evan. "PSSHAK." *RIBA Journal* (October), pp. 434–445, 1971.

Hawkins, R. R. and C. H. Abbe. *New House from Old: A Guide to the Planning and Practice of Housing Remodeling.* New York: McGraw-Hill, 1948.

Herbert, G. *The Dream of the Factory-Made House.* Cambridge, MA: MIT Press, 1984.

Kendall, S. "Europe's 'Matura Infill System' Quickly Routes Utilities for Custom Remodeling." *Automated Builder* (May), pp. 16–18, 1996.

"Levitt's 1950 House." *Architectural Forum,* vol. 92, no. 4 (April), pp. 136–137, 1950a.

Lu, R. "The Atwater Market Experiment" (design project; instructor, Avi Friedman). Montreal, PQ: McGill University School of Architecture Affordable Homes Program, 1999.

Ma, W., M. Noguchi, and R. Lu. "The Atwater Market Experiment" (design project; instructor, Avi Friedman). Montreal, PQ: McGill School of Architecture Affordable Homes Program, 1999.

MacDonald, D. *Democratic Architecture: Practical Solutions to Today's Housing Crisis.* New York: Whitney Library of Design, 1996.

Martel, A. and G. Ignazi. "An Experiment with Adaptable Housing at Montereau." *Industrialization Forum,* vol. 5, no. 5, pp. 59–64, 1974.

Noguchi, M. *User Choice and Flexibility in Japan's Prefabricated Housing Industry: A Case Study* (unpublished M.Arch. thesis). Montreal, PQ: McGill School of Architecture, 1999.

Olssen, B. *Flexible Dwellings in Block of Flats: A Study of an Experimental Block in Dissett Uppsala.* Sweden Statens Institute for Byggnadforskning, Stockholm, Report R22, 1970.

"One Room House." *Architectural Forum,* vol. 95 (June), pp. 163–165, 1951a.

Ou, Y. *The Evolution of Prefabricated Interior Components for Post-Occupancy Modification* (unpublished M.Arch. thesis). Montreal, PQ: McGill School of Architecture, 1999.

Oxman, R. *Flexibility in Supports: An Analysis of the Effect of Selected Physical Design Variables upon the Flexibility of Support Type Housing Systems* (unpublished D.Sc. thesis). Haifa, Israel: Technion-Israel Institute of Technology, 1977.

———, G. Herbert, and A. Wachman. "The Hierarchical Principle and Its Architectural Application." *Journal of Architectural Science,* pp. 33–38, 1984.

"Quantity Production Reaches the Home Builder." *Business Week* (March 26), p. 25, 1930.

Rabeneck, A. "Housing Flexibility/Adaptability?" *Architectural Design,* vol. 49, no. 2 (February), pp. 76–91, 1974a.

———. "The Structure of Space in Family Housing." *Progressive Architecture,* vol. 55 (November), pp. 102–107, 1974b.

————, D. Sheppard, and P. Town. "Housing Flexibility?" *Architectural Design,* vol. 48, pp. 698–727, 1973.

Ravetz, A. "PSSHAK, 18 Months On." *Architects' Journal* (February), pp. 425–439, 1980.

Riche, M. "Retirement's Life Style Pioneers." *American Demographics,* pp. 42–56, 1986.

Rios, A. and A. Friedman. "Residential Modification of Narrow Front Affordable Grow Homes in Montreal, Canada." *Open House International,* vol. 21, no. 2, pp. 4–17, 1996.

Roberts, C. J. B. "Home Buying U.S.A.: A Systems Analysis." *Industrialization Forum,* vol. 1, no. 3, pp. 35–40, 1970.

Rowe, P. G. *Making a Middle Landscape.* Cambridge, MA: MIT Press, 1991.

Rybczynski, W. and A. Friedman. "An Affordable Cottage." *Harrowsmith Canada,* vol. XIII, no. 6 (March/April), pp. 64–65, 1989.

S & L Co. Ltd. *House 55 (Nexis): Image Catalog.* Osaka, Japan: S & L Co. Ltd., 1997.

Schneider, F. (ed.) *Floor Plan Atlas: Housing.* Basel, Switzerland: Birkhäuser Verlag, 1994.

Schumacher, E. F. *Small Is Beautiful: A Study of Economics as if People Mattered.* Point Roberts, WA: Hartley & Marks Publishers, 1973.

Schweitzer, R. and M. W. R. Davis. *America's Favorite Homes.* Detroit, MI: Wayne State University Press, 1990.

Sekisui Chemical Co. Ltd. *Two-U Setsubi '99: Equipment Select Book.* Tokyo, Japan: Sekisui, 1999.

Sichelman, L. "HUD's Plan for Affordable Housing is Ready to Go into Mass Production." *Chicago Tribune* (September 6), 1987.

Sternthal, B. *Factors Influencing the Diffusion of Innovative Products in North American Building Firms* (unpublished M.Arch. thesis). Montreal, PQ: McGill School of Architecture, 1993.

"Tri-Level House. *Architectural Forum,* vol. 92, no. 4 (April), pp. 142–143, 1950b.

Wissinger, J. *The Best Kit Homes.* Princeton, NJ: Philip Lief Group, 1987.

World Commission on Environment and Development. *Our Common Future.* Oxford, UK: Oxford University Press, 1987.

Illustrations not listed have been created by the author and members of his design team.

Chapter 1
1.03, p. 5: after Deilmann et al. (1973)
1.05, p. 8: Courtesy of Kohler Corporation
1.06, p. 10: Hawkins and Abbe (1948)

Chapter 2
2.01, p. 22–23: *Architectural Forum* (1950a)
2.02, p. 25: *Architectural Forum* (1950b)
2.03, p. 26: *Architectural Forum* (1951a)
2.04, p. 27: *Architectural Forum* (1949)
2.05, p. 29: *House and Home* (1952)
2.06, p. 31: Friedman and Pantelopoulos (1996)
2.07, p. 34: after Oxman (1977)
2.08, p. 36–37: after *Floor Plan Atlas: Housing* (1994)
2.09, p. 38: after Olssen (1970)
2.10, p. 40: after Dirisamer et al. (1976)
2.11, p. 41: after Dirisamer et al. (1976)
2.12, p. 42: after Hamdi et al. (1971)
2.13, p. 43: after Martel and Ignazi (1974)
2.14, p. 44: after Rabeneck et al. (1973)
2.15, p. 46: after Kendall (1996)

Chapter 3
3.01, p. 52: Rowe (1991)

Chapter 4
4.02, p. 70: Alnemer et al. (1993)
4.03, p. 71: Friedman (1996)

The Next Home

Architect:	Avi Friedman
Design Team:	Jasmin S. Fréchette
	Cyrus M. Bilimoria
	David Krawitz
	Doug Raphael
Consultants:	R. Kevin Lee
	Julia Bourke
	Richard Gingras
	Vince Cammalleri
Contributors:	Maxwell Pau
	Rosemary Olson
Sponsoring Organizations:	Matériaux Cascades
	Canada Mortgage and Housing Corporation
	Natural Resources Canada
	Société d'habitation du Québec
	Fermco Industries Ltd.
	Ikea Canada
Years:	1995–1996

Home in a Box

Architect:	Avi Friedman
Assistant:	Joseph Lai
Years:	1997–1998

Choices in the Forest

Architects:	Avi Friedman
	Jean-Marie Lavoie
	Paul Brassard

Developers:	Jean-Marie Lavoie
	Paul Brassard
Years:	1997–2000

Universal Use

Architect:	Avi Friedman
Design Team:	José A. Martinez Di Bona
	Jasmin S. Fréchette
	Cyrus M. Bilimoria
	David Krawitz
	Monica Slanik
	Shawn Lapointe
	Hor Hooi Ping (Agnes)
Year:	1996

Avi Friedman received his Bachelor of Architecture degree from the Technion-Israel Institute of Technology, his Master of Architecture degree from McGill University, and his Ph.D. from the Université de Montréal. He cofounded the Affordable Homes Program at the McGill School of Architecture, where he is an Associate Professor.

Avi Friedman is the author of the books *The Grow Home* and *Planning the New Suburbia: Flexibility by Design*. He has written extensively on subjects ranging from prefabrication and construction technology to suburban planning and space management.

Dr. Friedman has worked as the head of design for a homebuilding firm in Montreal. He has designed housing prototypes that were constructed by home-builders in the private sector. The *Grow Home*, a narrow-front rowhouse, received immense media attention and has since been built in communities across North America. The *Next Home*, also the subject of much media scrutiny, is a flexible and affordable housing type. Dr. Friedman's design work and projects have been covered extensively on TV shows such as ABC's *Good Morning America*, *Dream Builders*, and Stewart Brand's *How Buildings Learn* (British Broadcasting Corporation), in magazines such as *Popular Science*, *Architecture*, and *Home*, and in newspapers including *The New York Times*, *Los Angeles Times*, and *San Francisco Examiner*. Avi Friedman has been a speaker at meetings of government officials, development authorities, university faculties and students, homebuilders, architects, and planners. He has received numerous awards for his research, design, and teaching, including the American Institute of Architects Education Honors, the Association of Collegiate Schools of Architecture Creative Achievement Award, the Progressive Architecture Research Award, the Manning Award for Technological Innovation, and the United Nations World Habitat Award.